SPEAK

SPEAK

Love Your Story.
Your Audience Is Waiting.

A teaching memoir by
Sally Lou Oaks Loveman

BALBOA.PRESS
A DIVISION OF HAY HOUSE

Balboa Press books may be ordered through booksellers or by contacting:

Balboa Press
A Division of Hay House
1663 Liberty Drive
Bloomington, IN 47403
www.balboapress.com
1 (877) 407-4847

Because of the dynamic nature of the Internet, any web addresses or
links contained in this book may have changed since publication and
may no longer be valid. The views expressed in this work are solely those
of the author and do not necessarily reflect the views of the publisher,
and the publisher hereby disclaims any responsibility for them.

The author of this book does not dispense medical advice or prescribe the use
of any technique as a form of treatment for physical, emotional, or medical
problems without the advice of a physician, either directly or indirectly. The
intent of the author is only to offer information of a general nature to help
you in your quest for emotional and spiritual well-being. In the event you use
any of the information in this book for yourself, which is your constitutional
right, the author and the publisher assume no responsibility for your actions.

Printed in the United States of America.

ISBN: 978-1-9822-3955-8 (sc)
ISBN: 978-1-9822-3953-4 (hc)
ISBN: 978-1-9822-3954-1 (e)

Library of Congress Control Number: 2019920254

Balboa Press rev. date: 01/02/2020

To the hearts that poured love into mine
and prepared me for a stage where my love speaks.

This is for you, Dad.

My stories are told as best as I remember them. Some names have been changed, but most have not because I believe names give our stories more power. That's a lesson I learned from the woman whose name I use the most. I hope my stories stick with you

Contents

Introduction

To have a career we love, to fall in love, to love ourselves, and to love our story, we have to be willing to do the hardest work of our lives. We have to love. When we live our lives with love, we become more comfortable with ourselves, and we feel more joy. We laugh more. We live more. We forgive more. We speak more. *SPEAK: Love Your Story. Your Audience Is Waiting* is a reminder that love wins.

Join me as I share my story and offer some laughs, some inspiration, some speaker tips, and a few life lessons too. The idea is to keep moving forward—whatever forward means for you. When we share our stories, we connect with others, and that connection makes us all happier humans. When we speak our stories, we share the moments of our lives that have shaped us, which connects us more deeply to others.

Our stories are our gifts, and when we share them with the people who surround us in life, we suddenly find ourselves speaking with more ease in daily conversations, in meetings, and even on stages. Using our voices to tell our stories removes fear from speaking and makes us more connected humans, which is the message of this book.

SPEAK is a love letter to my story and everyone in it. I believe in letting our love speak by loving our stories. If we don't love our stories and speak them, who else will?

In my wildest dreams, I never thought I would be capable of writing a book. I have had this ongoing chatter playing on a loop in my head. I've asked myself over and over, "Who would care about my story?" When I finally answered my inner doubter's voice, I said, "Me. I care." That's when I decided to commit to writing *SPEAK* and stopped using air quotes when I told someone I was writing a book.

I am not saying I have a perfect story. Trust me when I say I don't. I'm not saying I am a perfect human, because I'm not. I'm also not saying I am the best speaker you've ever heard. What I am saying is that we can all use some inspiration and that a good laugh never hurt anyone. There are many days when I need to read my own damn book!

What I do know is that at the root of all our stories is love, and when we speak our stories, we spread love. I hope you see yourself in some of my stories. I hope you connect with yourself more deeply. I hope you connect with people you love, or people you don't even know yet, when you finish. I hope you connect with me. If my book inspires you to sit down and write your story—or speak your story—I will consider that a huge victory.

Your story is a gift to yourself and to your family. It doesn't have to be a book. It just needs to be loved and shared. I have deep gratitude for anyone who cares enough to read my story because it means you are invested in your own.

For seasoned speakers and people who are scared to speak in public, I have you both covered. Step up your speaking game with my unexpected speaker tips I offer throughout the book, and get noticed on the stage, at work, and in your personal life. Or use my tips to help you find the courage to start somewhere.

Just like the preshow audience warm-up I performed as the audience producer for *The Oprah Winfrey Show*, this book is participatory. Each chapter ends with a prompt for you to add your own words and thoughts in order to help you start your own story and be a better speaker, be a better human, and live a better life. It is my hope that when you finish this book, you will have a beautiful start to your own story.

Finally, I have two unexpected gifts just for you. The first is an additional eighteen journal pages to take notes in the back of the book as you read along. In Hebrew, the number eighteen means life. These pages are for you to give life to your story and are specific to the practice you are about to begin. Use these pages to reference your work and your growth. Use these pages as a reminder to keep moving forward. Use these pages however they benefit you.

The second unexpected gift serves as a reminder to commit to the work. The section "Top Ten lovespeaks Lessons to Live By" can be posted anywhere you want to remind yourself to let love speak.

Thank you for joining me on this journey. Your love speaks!

Sally Lou

CHAPTER 1

The Unexpected Speaker

When we speak we are afraid our words will not be heard or welcomed.
But when we are silent, we are still afraid. So it is better to speak.
—AUDRE LORDE

I never expected to be a speaker. In fact, my nursery school teacher Mrs. Thompson told my mother that I would never make a friend because I was so shy. It wasn't the nicest thing for my teacher to tell my mother, and actually, it wasn't the nicest thing for my mother to tell me. I am not exactly sure how I found out this fun fact; but I assume my mom told me, and I remember it upset me. Mrs. Thompson's words stuck with me at a very early age, and I was determined not to give power to her label.

But the truth is that Mrs. Thompson wasn't completely wrong. I was shy. I never left my mother's side when I was young. I held onto her skirt or pant leg everywhere we went. It didn't help that my mom was a world-class practical joker and that I was easy prey.

When we rode the elevator at Strawbridge & Clothier, our local department store, the doors would close, and if no one else was in the elevator with us, my mom would break into a tap dance known as the buffalo shuffle. I was terrified and thought her dancing would stop the elevator in between floors. The doors would open, and she would walk out with full composure like nothing had happened. I would walk out shook.

One day when I got off the school bus from kindergarten, I ran down the hill to my house, and when I got to the front door, I screamed, "Mommy, I'm home!"

My mom replied, "I'm not your mother!" *Not funny.*

Trust me—I have discussed this at great length in therapy, and you would think my mom is really mean. She is actually just really funny. I had to grow up to learn this. My mom's humor is her gift. She needs absolutely no prep for her jokes, and she knows her audience—a skill I have made a living out of.

Luckily, I was able to move on to first grade without too much trauma and ended up graduating from high school with a homecoming queen title. There's no way Mrs. Thompson saw that coming. Nor did I!

But I still struggled in first grade, and I was scared of everything, especially Miss Baker. I couldn't be in the cafeteria when Miss Baker was the lunch lady. She would come over to every student's seat to make sure we had finished our lunches. We even had to tilt our milk cartons over to prove we had finished our milk. What made the whole thing even more terrifying was she used a microphone to announce our names if we hadn't finished. I wanted no part of this.

My mother called the principal's office and asked for Miss Baker's schedule, and on Miss Baker's days, my mom made me half a sandwich instead of a whole sandwich because my mom isn't mean. She's funny. But that wasn't enough. Just the sight of Miss Baker would make me lose my appetite. So I asked my first-grade teacher, Miss Brown, if I could stay in the classroom for lunch when Miss Baker was on duty, which meant I would miss recess too.

Miss Brown said yes, and I hid in my cubby in the classroom when I heard people go by in the hallway because I was embarrassed they might see me in my dark classroom. But there was no way I was going to risk Miss Baker coming over to me with her microphone to ask me if I had finished my lunch and my milk. Funny how I love a microphone now and have no problem finishing my breakfast, lunch, or dinner and always have room for dessert.

Around this same time when I was scared of everything, I promised my mom that I would never leave her and live with her forever. We all make stupid promises, and I definitely broke mine when I grew up and moved to Chicago right after college for a television job at the PBS station WTTW-TV. That was the same year Oprah Winfrey moved to Chicago to host a local morning show called *AM Chicago*.

Two years later Oprah took her local show national and launched *The Oprah Winfrey Show*. One year after that, I was hired as the show's audience coordinator. I was twenty-five years old when someone unexpectedly handed me a microphone and told me to warm up the studio audience. I had no idea what that meant, so I spoke from my heart, which was unexpected, and it worked. The audience was probably expecting a stand-up comic. Instead they got me. But if you know me, you know my dream of doing stand-up is real.

Having entertained more than half a million people from *The Oprah Winfrey Show* stage, this scared little girl grew up to perform the audience warm-up on the stages of Caesar's Palace, Radio City Music Hall, the Sydney Opera House forecourt, the Kodak Theatre (now the Dolby Theatre), Madison Square Garden Theater, Chicago's United Center, and a Michigan Avenue stage in Chicago where twenty-three thousand people showed up to learn a flash mob dance.

But in first grade I chose to hide in my cubby because Miss Baker terrified me. We all have a Miss Baker in our lives. I have had many more Miss Bakers in my professional life. Miss Baker prepared me for them, and I managed to survive most. It's okay to be afraid. It's not okay to stay in our cubbies.

If speaking in public scares you, get out of your *cubby* and take every opportunity to speak. Speak as much as you can until it becomes so routine that you no longer fear it. It will be uncomfortable—I get that. But our speaking experience accumulates, and every experience we have, no matter how big or small, counts. Each time we speak, we become more comfortable in front of an audience, and it grows from there.

As the audience producer for *The Oprah Winfrey Show*, I was never nervous to perform the audience warm-up because I was so caught up in my purpose—seating the audience—that it never dawned on me to be scared. Connecting with people, getting the audience into the studio safely and seating them quickly so we could start on time when rehearsals ran long, and meeting every challenge we faced along the way kept me from being too scared to speak to the audience.

I was so focused on the business of making hundreds, sometimes thousands of people happy that I forgot I would be speaking on a stage in front of them. That business of making people happy gave me an opportunity to make friends with the audience, and we are never scared to speak to our friends. My friendship with the audience made me a better speaker, and I realized others could benefit from my discovery.

As speakers, we want to avoid fear, and the easiest way to avoid fear is by mingling with our audience before we speak. Remember speaking is about the audience. It's not about us, which is why I believe getting to know our audience is at the heart of where a good speaker becomes a great speaker. It's all about the audience. Keep this in mind when you speak, and it will calm your fears.

When we speak, we focus on our part, the content of our speech, and that's okay. But we can't lose sight of the audience—what they take away from our speech as well as the energy they bring us. Mingling with the audience before we speak allows us to get to know these people and allows them to get to know us.

Think of "the mingle" like a red-carpet event without the "who are you wearing?" question—that is, unless you want to know who they are wearing, which is a legitimate mingle question. Ask audience members why they are there, who they brought, how their day is going, and what they hope to take away from your speech. Get a funny or meaningful anecdote from someone, and remember that person's name to use later in your speech. Names make every story or speech more memorable. Using people's names in your audience unexpectedly captures their attention and reminds your audience that they matter.

Gathering fun facts from your audience also allows you to incorporate *live* content into your speech, which connects you to your audience and shows them you can think fast on your feet. The mingle allows you to speak in real time, which makes you human and memorable.

We live in a real-time world with Twitter, Facebook Live, Snapchat, Instagram, and live streaming. As speakers, we need to speak in real time and incorporate what's happening in the room *live*. When people enter the room, greet them. If people have a reaction to something you've said, ask them to respond. If someone's phone rings, ask that individual who's calling. If someone sneezes, say, "God bless you." If your PowerPoint fails, wing it. Speaking on a stage doesn't mean you've lost your manners or that you can't have a human reaction. Be human, and connect with your audience just like you do when you are off of a stage.

Without the mingle, we are simply speakers in front of an audience. With the mingle, we are speakers in front of an engaged audience, and engaged audiences always make us better speakers.

Sometimes we aren't able to access our audience before we speak, and that's when we have to get creative. Find a way to mingle with a few people who haven't entered the room yet, or if you are doing a run-through or rehearsal, mingle with the people in the room who will be attending your speech. If there is a prefunction area before the event opens, mingle with your audience there. The ladies' room is my favorite place to work an audience. I have mingled more with my audiences in ladies' rooms than I have in ballrooms.

One time I was sweating right through a red cotton dress I was wearing and had to take it off in the ladies' room to dry my sweat marks under the hand dryer before I took the stage. There I was, standing in the ladies' room in my Spanx and mingling with my audience. Someone suggested I buy some mini pads in the hotel lobby sundry store and stick them in my armpits after my dress was dry for some added protection. So I did, and it worked.

If you are sweating, it means you are human. It doesn't mean you aren't ready. Just be prepared, and wear clothing that conceals your sweat. Jackets are usually safe. Black is always safe but not always the happiest color on a stage, so try to add a splash of color if you wear black.

Light clothing is not safe on stage. Light clothing needs a buffer. Sew sweat pads into light clothing as I had my dry cleaner do for me when I arrived home with my sweaty red cotton dress. Mini pads work, but if you want to reduce your fear of speaking, mini pads may increase your fear. The entire time I was speaking, I was worried one of the mini pads was going to fall out of my sleeve and land on the stage.

Thankfully the minipads stayed in place, and my sweaty speech happened to be one of my most powerful moments on a stage, proving that vulnerability has its perks. Be vulnerable when you speak, but it's also important to be prepared because nobody likes a sweaty speaker.

The mingle reduces fear. It warms us up. It invites an engaged audience, and it gives a speaker a safety net, and I haven't met a speaker yet who doesn't want a safety net. When we mingle with our audience before we speak and include our audience from the beginning of our speech, we can include them throughout our entire speech, which gives us, the speakers, a safety net.

Here's how it works. If you get lost, engage your audience while you get yourself back on track. Ask someone a question while you figure out what comes next in your speech. This gives you a little time to gather yourself. It seems perfectly normal because you have already engaged your audience when you started your speech, so asking your audience a question is not awkward.

It's not always easy to have a quick and authentic conversation with someone while you are thinking about what comes next in your speech, but when it works, it's magic. And I am a big fan of magic.

Don't try this "safety net" move the first time with too many people. Start with one person, and test the waters. Soon you will find yourself executing it naturally, which is what makes it authentic. This is my go-to "safety net" trick, and I use it every time I speak.

According to *The Book of Lists*, speaking in public is the number-one fear people have. People fear speaking in public over death, heights, and bugs. Jerry Seinfeld jokes that people would rather be in the coffin than deliver the eulogy. For some crazy reason, I managed to dodge the number-one fear people have, but I got stuck with all the others. I am afraid of planes, trains, boats, bridges, open water, elevators, self-park parking lots, amusement park rides, choking, and getting lost while driving just to name a few.

The only time I am fear-free is when I am on a stage with a microphone in front of hundreds or thousands of people. I know, I am not normal. But I want to help you not be normal too because normal is so expected.

Some of us will be asked to give keynotes, and some of us will not. But almost all of us will have an opportunity to tell our story, speak at a meeting, interview with a potential employer, take a meeting with our boss, present to our team, give a toast at a loved one's celebration, maybe even give a TED talk, teach an exercise or yoga class, or just be on Facebook Live. Each opportunity requires us to have excellent speaking and storytelling skills.

Speaking is like everything we do. It's a practice. It's just like yoga, exercise, meditation, prayer, reading, knitting, and playing mahjong or golf. You can fill in the blank for whatever it is you enjoy and consistently work at to get better. The more we speak, the more skilled we are at speaking, and since I have been at this practice for thirty-five years, I offer my stories, speaker tips, and life lessons to help you love your story too.

When we love our story, we remove fear from speaking in public, we engage our audience more easily, we speak from our heart, and we leave a little room for the unexpected, which is always extra.

So I invite you to speak! Speak up. Speak on stages. Speak your truth. Speak to your family. Speak to strangers. Speak kindly to yourself. Speak your story. Let go a little, and have fun when you speak. Don't be scared. Look forward to speaking. I want you to love speaking, no matter how big or small your stage is.

It doesn't matter what the size of your audience is. It matters that an audience has gathered to listen to *you*. Repeat that to yourself again. It matters that an audience has gathered to listen to *you*. Reward your audience by being who you are. Share your story, and enjoy the moment.

LOVESPEAKS LESSON #1: The unexpected lesson I learned as a young girl was to not let labels define me. I let them inspire me. If someone tells you that you can't do something or be something, prove to yourself that you can. Miss Baker wasn't sent to scare me. She was sent to inspire me. Mrs. Thompson wasn't sent to label me. She was sent to launch me.

This scared little girl grew up to be a speaker who spreads her message without fear, which means anyone can do what they dream of.

So welcome whoever your Miss Baker or Mrs. Thompson is in your life, and let them light a fire in you to help you grow and go after your dream. It's never about proving yourself to whoever your Miss Baker or Mrs. Thompson is. It's about proving yourself to you. Show yourself who you are by using all the talents you have been blessed with, and go after your dream. And when you accomplish your dream, share your story with your audience.

Always remember to look for the Miss Browns in your life too. There is always someone who can help you feel safe as you grow into who you really are. You just have to ask for their help. When women support women, labels don't exist.

What label did you overcome?

_____

_____

_____

LOVESPEAKS PRACTICE: Remind yourself of your purpose every morning before your feet hit the floor. Write your purpose down. Ask yourself how your purpose serves you and how it serves others. Let this practice serve as a reminder that when you are in your purpose, you can do anything because fear has no access.

ALTERNATIVE LOVESPEAKS PRACTICE: If this sounds like too much for you, remind yourself that tomorrow is coming. So is next week, next month, and next year. You will get there. We don't have to all arrive in our purpose or overcome labels at the same pace. We just have to move forward. Moving forward is different for everyone. Be okay with whatever forward means for you.

LIVE LOVESPEAKS: Because I am afraid to fly, you know what I do? I move forward with my fear and fly all the time. I am a frequent flyer. I hate it, but I do it. It's called practice. In fact, a lot of this book, and many of my speeches and workshops were written on an airplane.

And that's the message I want to send to you. Whether you are a comfortable speaker or an uncomfortable one, take every opportunity to speak, no matter how uncomfortable it makes you, and soon you'll be walking up to a microphone on a stage like I board a plane, almost cocky.

I was speaking at an event for my favorite airline, and one of their pilots was being honored for his excellent care of his passengers and crew. I gave him a little "You've got this" tap on his shoulder when he was called up to the stage to accept his award.

I could see him shaking on the stage from my seat, and I thought to myself, *This man flies 737s and is responsible for nearly a thousand lives each week.* I wanted to scream, "Captain, you've got this!" It made absolutely no sense to me.

And yet we all have our fears. If I were flying a 737, I would be shaking too. Obviously, pilots have to be trained to fly a plane, but people have to be trained to speak. We have to be trained for anything we do. Part of getting over something we fear is doing the very something that we fear over and over again.

We train. We practice. We conquer.

Even though I appear calm when I fly, I experience that gut-wrenching ball of stress every time I board a plane. I always say the same prayer when I board, and when we take off, I go through all the same rituals. I recite more prayer. I repeat my children's names. I hold onto my cross, and sometimes I resort to curling up in the fetal position, which completely blows my cover.

My fear is real. It goes back to when I was sixteen years old and almost died in a small plane. We got caught in an August storm, which felt more like a hurricane, but back then we called them storms. I was on the plane with my best friend, Betsy, my father (who hated to fly), and the pilot.

We took off in sunny blue skies, but an hour into the flight, we hit a storm, and the plane lost its instruments. I remember the pilot's face. It was slammed against the windshield. The squeaky windshield wiper went back and forth, doing absolutely nothing to help with visibility.

I started to chant. I didn't know what chanting was, but suddenly, I was chanting. The sound of my voice soothed me. It was like a hum in my head that calmed me down. I was chanting *om* before I even knew what *om* was.

We were heading to Philadelphia, and we were very lucky to make an emergency landing in Atlantic City, New Jersey, at Bader Field, a small municipal airport. When we walked off that plane, I knew I would never like to fly again, but I also knew I had discovered a spiritual power that could only come from one place. From that day forward, I walked with God.

The chance of me ever boarding a plane with a skip and a smile was slim to none, but being the frequent flyer that I am, I fake that skip and smile every time I board a plane. Don't let fear keep you from speaking. When you feel your nerves churning in your stomach, it doesn't mean you're not ready or not a great speaker. It means you are human. And human is a good thing.

We all get nervous. Instead of allowing your nerves to take control and keep you from speaking, use your nerves as motivation to push you forward. Picture the inside of your stomach like butterflies, and let the power of their wings lift you up, not take you down. Chant if you have to.

I always write on an airplane because writing and sharing my story as a speaker is my purpose. When I'm in my purpose, fear has no access. Whatever your purpose is, use it to keep fear as far away from you as possible.

What is your purpose?

_____

_____

_____

CHAPTER 2

A Little Bit of Extra Love Goes a Long Way

The human voice is the most perfect instrument of all.
—ARVO PÄRT

We all have a story. Some of us tell our story really well. Some of us don't tell it at all. And some of us could use a little help. Whatever category you fall into, you deserve to love your story, own your story, and speak your story. Whether you are sharing your story with an audience of one, a hundred, or a hundred thousand, your story matters, and you should never underestimate the impact your story has on someone else. Our stories are what connect us. They remind us that we are more alike than we are unalike, which gives us all permission to own our stories, love our stories, write our stories, and speak our stories.

A group of neuroscientists at Princeton University did a study that revealed storytelling makes us happier humans. Don't we all want to be happier humans?

When we hear a story that we can relate to, our levels of oxytocin increase, which is why oxytocin is often referred to as the "feel good" hormone. Stories allow us to feel more compassion, have more trust, and encourage more empathy. In other words, our stories make us more human.

Johnathan Gottschall, the author of *The Storytelling Animal: How Stories Make Us Human*, says, "We are, as a species, addicted to story. Even when the body goes to sleep, the mind stays up all night, telling itself stories."

In my quest to be a better human, I decided to tell my story and write a book. For the past five years, I've been writing my story in my head, in my phone, in my dreams, in my computer, on my blog, in my notebook, on napkins, and on scraps of paper. I have been mentored by several successful women author friends and have had different titles along the way.

Frankly, I was getting sick of talking about my book, and I'm pretty sure my friends were getting sick of hearing about it too. When I finally committed to putting all my notes together in one place, Michelle Obama's book *Becoming* was being released, which I fully took as a sign it was time to actually write mine.

Michelle Obama is one of my speaker heroes (of the four I have) because she speaks from her heart, she is genuinely herself, she compliments and thanks her audience, she allows her audience to finish her sentences (which is a total rock-star move), and she is unexpected. When she tells her "Bye, Felicia" story, I fall in love with her even more—if that's possible.

It's important to have a speaker hero, even if you never meet or work with your hero. That doesn't mean we can't claim certain people and call upon them to motivate us through their social media, their books, and their television appearances. I am not the first person to claim Michelle Obama as my speaker hero, but I can say that in 2012, I introduced the former First Lady before she took the stage to speak.

It was just one of the many magical moments I was privileged to have while working at Harpo Studios. As the First Lady of the United States stood next to me backstage in her white pantsuit, towering over me like a superhero woman, I felt the power of her story. I can only describe the moment as electric. When I said, "Ladies and gentlemen, please welcome the First Lady of the United States, Michelle Obama," my knees went completely weak.

When *Becoming* arrived at my front door, I turned to the back cover and saw Michelle Obama's quote "Your story is what you have, what you will always have. It is something to own." *Yes! Yes! Yes!* Michelle Obama was speaking my language, and I was already feeling more human.

That evening as I sat in the audience at the United Center in Chicago and listened to Michelle Obama speak, I couldn't help but think that the universe had put me exactly where I was supposed to be. Michelle Obama was speaking her story and reminding us all how important our stories are, the very message of my book. Love was speaking, and I was listening.

Chicago was the first city on Michelle Obama's stadium book tour, and Oprah Winfrey (speaker hero number two) was the celebrity to kick it off. While I desperately wanted to be working the event, I sat in my seat and tried to take it all in just like everyone else. I couldn't help but remember what it felt like to be on that United Center stage as the audience producer for *The Oprah Winfrey Show* in front of fifteen thousand people, performing the audience warm-up for *Oprah's Twenty-Fifth Season Surprise Spectacular*. I closed my eyes and told myself, "Just be in the moment, Sally Lou."

It was hard for me, but I managed. So much so that at one point I thought Michelle Obama was actually going to speak my book title. I pulled up my notes in my phone to show my girlfriend Cindy, as evidence that I wasn't crazy. Love was speaking, oxytocin was pumping and all I had to do was write my damn book.

I may add a little extra to my stories and be a little dramatic and go beyond what is usual or expected, like Michelle Obama speaking my book title, but the reality is that at the heart of every story, there is truth, whether a little extra has been added or not. And when that truth is shared by someone out there who has a similar story, that person feels validated through yours. Michelle Obama was validating my book because she was loving her story, plain and simple.

Oprah Winfrey taught us all that people just want to be seen and heard and know they matter. Oprah also taught us that everyone has a story. I was very lucky to have had a front-row seat not only to Oprah's powerful story but also to the stories that were told on *The Oprah Winfrey Show* that changed the world. As the audience producer for *The Oprah Winfrey Show*, I was the opening warm-up act for the show, and I loved my job with all my heart. Today I am just another woman telling my story and wanting to be a better human.

But I will always leave a little room for extra because extra is unexpected. My family and I play a game I like to call "What Celebrity Said This to Mommy?" When I say family, I really just mean me since I'm the one who made up the game and my kids don't participate—that is, unless you call eye-rolling participation. My kids are not always my best audience. But then again, I am a lot to live with, and I can be very extra.

When I took a photo with Denzel Washington backstage at *The Oprah Winfrey Show*, he asked me, "Why are you blushing, Sally?" That is why Denzel Washington is the only human I allow to call me Sally. Welcome to me being extra.

When I forgot to distribute Hall of Fame and baseball great Cal Ripken Jr.'s books to the studio audience after he was a guest on the show, Cal Ripken extended his enormous hand backstage to me as I was lugging heavy boxes of his books to the studio, and then he said, "Let me help you. I'm retired."

I told Diane Keaton she was beautiful as she walked by me before she made her entrance on the show, and she replied, "What? You look just like me!" I was dressed in black and wearing my glasses, so maybe that's what prompted her to put me in her category, but I'm not about to keep her comment out of the game.

Andy Samberg said, "Nice headset," when he caught me in the studio leading a meeting with my team before our audience load, acting like I was solving the world's biggest problems.

I ran into Wynonna Judd in the ladies' room after she was a guest on the show, and as we were washing our hands, she told me I was sassy, which I took as a complete and total compliment.

And after a full day of working with the late great Whitney Houston, an artist I have loved since the day she released "I Wanna Dance with Somebody," Whitney placed her magnificent hands on my pregnant stomach and sang with her Grammy-winning voice, "Bless you, baby," to my son Billy, who was in utero and who happens to have a beautiful voice. I always remind Billy that Whitney Houston gave him his voice because that's what extra people do.

I could go on with my game, but I won't because I fear you will roll your eyes too. So here's the truth. Yes, celebrities always make for a better story. Anything extra does. But it was the regular people like you and me who told their stories on *The Oprah Winfrey Show* who left the biggest imprint on my heart. And that is what this book is about—you and me and our stories. The extra is ... extra.

I happen to love my story, and I want you to love your story. I hold onto my story like I used to hold on to my baby blanket, which I still would hold on to if it was socially acceptable. My story is my comfort, my joy, and my security, including the parts that are ugly and painful. Somehow I have found a way to love those parts too because there is always something to learn. It's when we grow and hopefully thrive.

Some of the stuff that happens to me I couldn't even begin to make up if I tried. Every Monday morning I would walk into my office at Harpo Studios, armed with a *Living Loveman* story to share with my audience team. *Living Loveman* is what we called my fake reality show, and I always had a segment-one story to tell. All television producers know that the juiciest story is the segment-one story.

For example, there was the time I forgot to check my daughters' passports before they were leaving with friends who had generously invited them to Mexico for spring break. My girls were in high school, and I was never off for spring break, so I got very lucky when our daughters' friends invited them to join them on vacation. I totally screwed up when I discovered the Friday night before they were leaving (just two days away) that their passports were expired and the passport offices were generally not open on the weekend.

But we are the stars of *Living Loveman*, so somehow we managed to find an open office. It just happened to be in another state. Four planes later my husband arrived home with our daughters' passports just in time for them to leave for the airport. That sounds super privileged, and truthfully, it totally is.

But for me, it is just another example of what happens to working moms who are trying to keep it together, and more often than not, we find ourselves losing the battle. There were so many things that fell through the cracks when I was working seventy-hour work weeks. This story just happens to be the most ridiculous one.

I missed picking up my kids from school and being home to help them with their homework. I missed so many school activities, and I always had work on my mind. If you are like me, you resort to doing things that are completely out of your budget to clean up the mess you make when things are missed, which is never good for anyone.

The upside to me messing up as a parent is that I was able to laugh about my failures with my team most Monday mornings. My team was always in the front row for my stories, and I never seemed to run short of material. Not only were my teammates the best audience bookers in the business, but they were also my best audience. I miss that.

My audience is now our Yorkshire Terrier rescue dog Gracie, whom I love with all my heart. Prior to Gracie, my audience was our beloved Shih Tzu, Tinker, which pretty much sums up what it's like to work without a team. It can be very lonely, and while I love my dogs, I crave group laughter.

The *Harvard Business Review* says, "Stories create sticky memories by attaching emotions to things that happen." We want our stories to stick, so don't be scared to love your story, even the parts you wish you didn't have to tell. Trust me—*Living Loveman* has a chapter or two I struggle with. The only way through the parts of our story we struggle with is to share those parts with the people who have earned the right to hear them, even if those individuals are dogs.

Or you can write a book like me if you are brave enough and want to help others. And if you are really brave and you want to make people laugh, you can write and perform a stand-up comedy act about your story. I wrote my stand-up act five years ago and have never performed it because I am not brave enough … yet. It lives in my phone notes and predates *The Marvelous Mrs. Maisel*. Let's just say Midge and I could have a laugh.

The lesson is that our stories literally save us. So love your story, write your story, and speak your story. Add extra where needed.

LOVESPEAKS LESSON #2: Our stories are what connect us to our audience. When you are speaking to an audience, use your voice as an instrument, and include content from your own life that relates to the topic you are speaking about so you can quickly capture your audience and assure them you are the real deal and someone they can trust. Get the oxytocin pumping as soon as you take the stage.

Sharing part of your story builds trust with your audience. The story you share makes you an expert on whatever topic you are speaking about. It also makes you a better human. Your story will stick with your audience, and so will the feeling they had when you were sharing that part of you that only you can share. It's the unexpected gift your audience gets to take home. And don't forget to give them a little extra for fun.

What is your favorite story to tell?

_____

_____

_____

LOVESPEAKS PRACTICE: Share a story with someone. It doesn't matter if it's your coworker, a family member, your best friend, or a stranger. Share a story with someone, and feel your connection deepen with the human race. Reward yourself by writing down the story you shared as a reminder that it's your favorite.

Maybe you heard a story that made an impact on you? Make a note of that too. Begin to collect your stories in one place. This can be your own private book that serves as an excellent resource for you when you are ready to speak.

ALTERNATIVE LOVESPEAKS PRACTICE: If you are not ready to share your story, practice listening. Notice how other people tell their stories and make note of what you like. When you are ready, let your notes be your guide on how you would like to speak.

LIVE LOVESPEAKS: My favorite story to tell is about my grandmother. She was a huge influence in my life. My grandmother was a master tea-sandwich maker. She didn't just make tea sandwiches. She created works of art.

Armed with an assortment of cookie cutters ranging from baby carriages to umbrellas, no tea sandwich left my grandmother's house until it was properly decorated with her signature design she delicately applied with an icing gun filled with food-colored cream cheese. Her dainty flowers and intricate ribbons made the ordinary cucumber tea sandwich come alive with its own love story of how it was created.

Tea sandwiches are not as popular today as they were when I was growing up—that is, unless you are having tea at a fancy hotel. I'm not even sure kids my age knew what tea sandwiches were in the 1970s, but in my world tea sandwiches were everything. I used to sit in my grandmother's living room on hot summer afternoons, smelling of OFF! bug spray while my legs stuck to the furniture, waiting for my grandmother's customers to arrive at her front door to pick up their orders.

The doorbell was notification that someone was about to add more love to their bridal shower, baby shower, birthday, or Easter celebration. It didn't matter what the occasion was. Those tea sandwiches packed an extra punch of love, which is why people kept showing up day after day to bring them home to their families.

My grandmother's story impacts me every day of my life. It motivates me to give more love to my family, my business, my relationships, my story, my audience, strangers, and new people I meet daily. I can hear her sweet voice encouraging me to stick to my purpose and spread love. I replay her story over and over again in my head as a reminder that love speaks.

Whoever inspires you, replay their stories, and let them fill you up in a way that serves your purpose. When we share our stories, not only do we connect with others and the people who came before us, but we also connect with ourselves. Our stories allow us to live more joyful lives, allow us to be better humans, and help us and others heal.

Who reminds you to love your story?

_____

_____

_____

CHAPTER 3

Accept Invitations from Your Mother

The tongue can paint what the eyes can't see.
—CHINESE PROVERB

Before we love our stories and speak our stories, we should know how to start our stories. So here's my challenge: How would you start your story in ten words or less? What are the words you would choose to capture who you are and your purpose?

It's a little daunting to have to catalog everything we have ever done in our lives and come up with a snappy sentence that sums us all up. But if we don't have a start our story, how will we speak our story?

I start my story with "accept invitations from your mother," and here's why: When I was fourteen years old, my mother took me to the filming of *The Mike Douglas Show.* It was one of the first talk shows on television, and it happened to be filmed in my hometown of Philadelphia. I skipped field hockey practice to go to the show, and as I sat in the studio audience, I spotted a girl on the set with a clipboard.

I didn't know what she did, but she was a woman. (It was 1976 by the way.) She was wearing a headset, which made her automatically cool, and she was carrying a clipboard, which made her automatically official. Plus she looked really busy. I knew in that moment that whatever it was she was doing, I would do it one day too.

I loved being in a television studio. I loved the smell of the studio, hearing the clicking sounds of the lights, the feel of the camaraderie of the crew, the sight of all the action, and the taste of the excitement. I quickly learned that when an environment sucks you in and pleases all five of your senses, you should make a career out of it.

A few months later, I went back to *The Mike Douglas Show,* but this time I was the one who asked my mother to get tickets because the stars from

Welcome Back, Kotter, a hit show in the '70s, were scheduled to be guests. John Travolta played the sexy Vinnie Barbarino, and he also happened to be my pretend boyfriend. His poster hung in my bedroom where I spent a lot of time listening to his records on repeat.

Somehow my mom got tickets again, and there we were, back in the studio audience, waiting to see the love of my life in the flesh. I brought Betsy because I wanted her to be part of my new television world. Suddenly a producer came out to tell us that sadly, John Travolta had canceled at the last minute—an early sign that television can sometimes be heartbreaking.

Even though the actor who played Freddy Washington came into the audience and kissed me on my cheek, I left the studio in tears. But I held on to the image of the girl with the clipboard throughout my high school years, and I even took her to college because I was determined to work in television one day just like her. I can still picture her in my mind, standing off to the right of the set under the show mezzanine, wearing a faded pair of jeans, long, straight hair, and no makeup.

The girl with the clipboard was a mentor I never met, and she remains my mentor today. Trust me—I have tried to find her through countless Google searches, and a few of my friends even thought they might have had a lead. But so far I have not been successful, so if you were on the production team or crew of *The Mike Douglas Show* in 1976, please help me make my reunion dream come true!

It's so easy for us to say no to an invitation from our mothers or from anyone who loves or likes us. I could have told my mom I had too much homework or didn't want to miss field hockey practice. None of us want to say yes to something that takes us out of our comfort zones or pulls us away from Netflix. Parents, you know what I'm talking about.

How many of you have heard no from your kids when you've invited them somewhere? I know so many of you are nodding your heads yes right now. And how many of you have said no to your mother when you were a kid … or worse, now?

What if the invitation you say no to is the one thing that could change the trajectory of your life like my mother's invitation changed mine? Or what if it's the one thing that could lead you to finding your story?

Saying no is like saying you don't care about your story. When I spoke at the Advancing Women in Trucking conference, an industry dominated by men, I ended my speech by saying, "Remember—girls are watching." When I said these words, I felt their power.

And guess what I found out after my speech? Boys are watching too. And mothers are not the only people with invitations. Fathers also have invitations. After my speech a man in the audience (one of only two) told me he realized he was *a dad with an invitation*. He said he had recently asked his twenty-one-year-old son, who had a passion for photography, to come along with him to a trucking event because they didn't have a photographer.

His son said yes for one reason. He knew there would be free beer at the end of the day! It doesn't matter why we say yes. It's that we say yes! This man's son did such a great job and enjoyed the work so much that opportunities began flowing his way for more photography work.

We are never too old to discover the one thing that drives us and defines our stories, and saying yes to an invitation from someone who loves or likes you—your mother, father, sister, brother, boss, or best friend—could be the key to unlocking the start of your story.

Author and researcher Brené Brown (speaker hero number three) says, "We are wired for story." Knowing where to begin our stories is sometimes the hardest part for most of us. So I invited some inspiring women friends of mine to share how they would start their stories in ten words or less, and luckily, they said yes!

Meet Bela. Bela Gandhi is a mother of two and founder and CEO of Smart Dating Academy. Bela starts her story by saying, "I love love. I love people. I love helping people find love." Okay, I gave Bela two extra words because I am a sucker for love.

I met Bela at a dinner hosted by Carol Bernick Lavin, former CEO of Alberto Culver and author of a beautiful book *Gather as You Go*. The room was filled with women who all have powerful stories. Bela came right up to me and said, "Hi, Sally Lou," and it was love at first sight. I completely appreciated Bela's use of my full name, and I was thrilled to have someone to talk to. Bela is known to have a sixth sense about people, and she was flexing her talent with me!

Prior to starting Smart Dating Academy, Bela was a top executive at a large multinational corporation that focuses on chemistry (the science kind). Having always had a talent for connecting people, Bela shifted gears and decided to use her love of chemistry in a whole new way, the chemistry of people.

Today Bela's warmth and insight makes searching for love fun, efficient, and most importantly, successful. Bela's love for love and love for people makes her the perfect person to help others find their love stories. Bela loves her story like it's her job because it literally is.

Once you have a start to your story, you can begin to love your story, which allows you to own not only your story but also your talents. When we think of our talents as things that can be shared, we own our talents more easily, which benefits everyone. Bela's talent is her sixth sense, which she uses in her role as matchmaker, and she has made a career out of helping hundreds of thousands of people find love.

I am a connector. That's my talent. I connect people. When I was a young girl, I liked connecting things, especially puzzles. I like when things fit neatly together. I like setting a beautiful table and putting together an outfit—talents I inherited from my mother. I am also in love with my label maker, iron, vacuum, and stain removers, and I like to weed. I like results that are immediate and tidy.

On my first day of seventh grade at Welsh Valley Junior High School, I wore a navy and white sweater set, a navy kilt, navy knee socks, and navy Hush Puppy shoes. Three local grade schools merged into one junior high school, and everyone in my new homeroom was wearing skin-tight low-cut jeans they'd bought from a store called Cliffhanger, jeans that were lovingly called cliffy low-cuts.

Along with their cliffy low-cuts, the kids in my homeroom were wearing huckapoo shirts that were just as tight as their jeans and made of polyester, a fabric I had not met yet. Let's just say I was not groovy.

I was terrified of everyone. No one looked like me or acted like me. Later, some of these groovy kids would become some of my best friends, a lesson on how to build your team. If you want your dream to work, your team can't look like you, think like you, or act like you. Our differences make us all stronger.

When I was six years old, I used to beg my older sisters Susan and Cindy to pretend they were celebrities so I could interview them on our reel-to-reel tape recorder. I spent a lot of time in my basement putting shows together with them. Susan played the guitar and sang beautifully, so she usually played Joni Mitchell or Judy Collins. Cindy usually played a beautiful celebrity like Jane Fonda or Elizabeth Taylor.

My sisters would turn the tables and interview me too. I remember tapping my fingers on the tape recorder to make it sound like we were in a newsroom. My sister Susan would say, "You're wasting tape, Loulie," if I went too long with an answer. That's what we worried about back then. Now we worry about our iCloud storage. I would replay the interviews over and over again, and I remember thinking to myself, *I really like this.* Storytelling felt good to me at a very young age.

In my television and speaking career, I used my talent for connecting things and started to connect people. Seating *The Oprah Winfrey Show* audience was like a giant puzzle for me, a puzzle with people. One empty seat made me crazy. It was just like a missing piece of a puzzle or a missing place setting at a table or—God forbid—an outfit that doesn't match.

When I seat a studio audience, I feel like I am putting together a magnificent masterpiece. Each person's energy and outfit becomes a part to the whole. I used to call the audience Skittle Nation because their outfits represented every color of the rainbow. My preshow warm-up became the show I created in my basement with my sisters but with real people. If connection was an art, it would be my medium because connection is my talent.

I love connecting our talents to the careers we choose because it makes us so much more efficient. It reduces the time wasted in trying to figure out who we want to be. We will spend a little more time on this in the next chapter because being efficient is something we can all benefit from in the same way we benefit from our stories. A great hack to finding your talent if you're stumped is to keep track of the compliments you receive. Behind every compliment is a talent waiting to be revealed.

LOVESPEAKS LESSON #3: Define your talent so you can use your talent and share it with others. Care for your talent because it is your gift. Whether your talent is puzzle-making, sandwich-making, or matchmaking, happy people who make careers out of their talents and share their talents with others are always prepared speakers and storytellers and usually pretty fabulous humans.

When you think of your talent as something that can be shared, you own it more easily. The best thing about doing what you love and sharing your talent with others is that it isn't selfish. It's the most generous thing you can offer the world because it benefits everyone.

What is your talent?

_____

_____

_____

LOVESPEAKS PRACTICE: Define what your talent is and own it daily. Speak it into the universe, and write it down. When you speak your talent or write your talent down on paper, it becomes real, and suddenly, you find yourself using your talent to make a positive impact on your own life and on others.

Once you own your talent, speak of it like it's your best friend. Don't be shy about it. It is a disservice to others if you keep your talent hidden. It's a disservice to yourself. It's also inefficient.

Make a point to ask people what their talent is. It's a small question that can build a world of connection, support, and friendship. Sometimes people can't see their own talents. When we ask others what their talents are, it literally makes people stop and take stock of what they have to offer the world, which reminds us all to share the talents we've been blessed with.

Practice accepting unexpected invitations from people who love or like you, even if the invitation is to something you have zero interest in. In fact, the less interest you have, the more reason to say yes. When you really want to say no, let that be your reminder to open your world up to new things and say yes.

ALTERNATIVE LOVESPEAKS PRACTICE: If you are not an extrovert like I am, I don't expect that any of this feels comfortable to you. You have other gifts. Find those gifts and share them with people you are comfortable with. The idea is to share your talent in your own way. Sharing is the first step to owning your talent and being brave enough to accept invitations from someone who loves or likes you. Sharing allows for more giving and more receiving.

LIVE LOVESPEAKS: Sometimes the universe sends you an invitation that changes your life. I wasn't looking for one, but that's when invitations unexpectedly find us. I had no idea saying yes to my mom's invitation at fourteen would lead me to a career in television and a front-row seat to the extraordinary world of Oprah Winfrey. Pay attention. Say yes. Allow people to impact your life without expectation.

At the age of four, my son Billy, the one who got his voice from Whitney Houston, said to me, "I want to be the guy who punches the buttons to make television shows when I grow up." Most four-year-old kids don't speak like this, but Billy is my lovespeaks child, so this is his language.

I hadn't even taken him to *The Oprah Winfrey Show* set yet, and he was already speaking like a professional. Even though he didn't know what a technical director was at the time, he sure described exactly what a technical director does. There was no denying his passion.

As Billy got older, he had opportunities to be on set, run camera, and hold a boom microphone. He was twelve years old when my dear friend and stage manager Bob McGowan put a headset on Billy and asked him to help bring a gospel choir onto *The Oprah Winfrey Show* stage.

This was an invitation into a world Billy wanted to be in, and it was a turning point for him. Today Billy loves blocking a scene on a stage, performing as an actor, being behind a camera, and directing. When his headset is on, Billy becomes very powerful. Bob lit that fire in Billy the way the girl with the clipboard lit mine. I will always be grateful to Bob. May he rest in peace.

In 2016, I invited Billy to see Garry Marshall speak at Northwestern University. Our friend and Northwestern graduate executive produced the film *Mother's Day* with Garry Marshall and generously invited us to a screening of the film. My son Billy said no to my invitation when I asked him to join us.

He didn't even have a good reason for saying no. Garry Marshall, a TV and film legend, spoke to the audience and described in detail what it takes to be an actor for the stage, for television, and for the big screen. We hung on Garry Marshall's every word and had the great privilege of meeting him after his talk. Billy would have met Garry Marshall too.

Billy gets it now, but that doesn't mean he will always say yes to me. But at least he knows that saying no can sometimes keep us from really cool things that could change the trajectory of our lives. It's a lesson I continue to remind all my children of—and myself as well.

We are never too old to discover the one thing that drives us. Our stories are always developing. We don't have to be fourteen to say yes to our mothers. We can be fifty-seven when our world suddenly opens up in a whole new way. Say yes to the next invitation you receive, and start a new chapter to your story.

Lame excuses are lame. They add nothing extra to our stories. Say yes to your mother's invitation. I don't care if it's lunch at Applebee's. Say yes to your mother because mothers know best.

I said yes to an invitation
from _____

where I
discovered _____,

and now
I am _____.

How would you start your story? Answer in ten words or less?

_____

_____

_____

CHAPTER 4

I'm Sensing a Story

The five senses are the ministers of our soul.
—LEONARDO DA VINCI

I love asking people what their talents were as young children and what environments please their five senses because whatever pleases our senses always leads us to careers we love. When we use our talents in careers we love, we are usually happier humans, and that often makes us better speakers.

My puzzle-making, interview-taking, *Mike Douglas Show* awakening put me on my career path and into the hands of the greatest mentor on earth, Oprah Winfrey. We can't plan for this. It can only happen when we are in complete alignment with the talents we have been blessed with and when we use those talents in an environment that pleases all five of our senses.

Think about your own formula. You may have never made the connection before. It's kind of cool to take stock of where you are today in your career and why. Or it's a great hack to finding a career if you are looking for one. It's also efficient.

When we add the innate talents we had as young people to an environment that pleases all five of our senses, we have what I call lovespeaks careers and lovespeaks stories. When something you love speaks to you, do that something. When we listen to our calling, our work becomes effortless.

Choosing our career doesn't have to be so complicated. Sometimes we make it complicated. To uncomplicate our careers, we must rely on our senses to lead us to an environment we love where we can use our greatest talents.

Smell

If I hadn't discovered a television studio when I was fourteen years old, I probably would have become a buyer at Bergdorf Goodman because I love the smell of leather goods and the feel of a purchase with an employee discount. I also love a well-merchandised store. Every time I am in New York City, I ride the escalator at Bergdorf Goodman, close my eyes, take a deep breath through my nose, and smile.

Meet Henry. My favorite lovespeaks career story is from my friend and family member Henry Harteveldt. Henry says he loved the smell of jet fuel when he was a young boy. His father traveled a lot for business, and whenever an airline or travel agent sent his dad a model of a plane, Henry says he would nab it. Henry took every opportunity to go to the airport to see his dad off on a trip or meet his dad when he arrived.

Growing up in Manhattan, Henry collected the timetables from the different airlines' ticket offices that lined NYC's Fifth and Madison Avenues. Henry says, "At the time, most boys my age had subscriptions to *Sports Illustrated* or *Playboy*. I subscribed to *Aviation Week & Space Technology* or *Flying* and had posters from TWA, Pan Am, and other airlines of their 747s all over my bedroom walls." Henry learned how to fly a plane before he knew how to drive a car, and today Henry is a leading analyst for the travel industry and is an expert on air travel.

I was lucky to be hired to speak on the farewell flight of United's 747, and of course, Henry was one of the special guests on board. I truly felt like I was traveling with a celebrity. Talk about love speaking. Henry and his aviation friends spoke a language I didn't understand, but I didn't need to because love always translates no matter what language we speak, even if the language is aviation.

Henry recently sent me a *New York Times* article featuring Michael J. Fox, who said that the smell of an arc light reminded him of being an actor. Smells create so much magic and so many memories in our lives and in our careers. The smell of Oprah's flatiron and hairspray reminds me of my purpose because it meant it was show day, a day when we would be transforming lives.

What smell reminds you of your purpose?

_____

_____

_____

Feel

Meet Val. My friend Val Haller, mother of four and one of the coolest grandmothers I know, is the founder of ValsList, a music concierge service that provides cutting-edge music for busy people. Val used to make music mixes for her friends and family as a teenager, and she remembers every family event by the music she played on the stereo.

Val says she does more than hear music. She feels music. When she went to college, she meticulously organized her music collection, which always rode with her in the front seat of her car.

At age fifty, Val turned her talent into a business when she launched ValsList. Today, her playlist company helps people find new music, and in her spare time, she also produces live music events. She recently launched the Winnetka Music Festival, a successful music festival in Winnetka, Illinois.

What do you feel more than most people?

_____

_____

_____

Hear

Meet Katie. My children's eighth-grade English teacher, Katie Geier, tears up when she hears people speak with proper grammar. She literally gushes over hearing people use direct and indirect objects correctly. I'm not even sure if I know what a direct object or indirect object is, but Mrs. Geier sure does. Katie loved playing school as a young girl and fulfilled her dream of becoming an English teacher.

What sound makes you gush?

_____

_____

_____

See

When I was speaking at an event in New York City, I met a woman who told me that when she was a young girl, she helped her mother, who was a housekeeper at a hotel, clean rooms. One day she saw a woman coming out of a hotel room carrying a briefcase, and in that moment she knew she would never become a housekeeper like her mother.

Instead she became a senior executive in the field of human resources. When she told me her story, I thanked her. Seeing the woman with a briefcase inspired her the same way the girl with the clipboard inspired me.

Who or what did you see as a young child that influenced your professional career as an adult?

_____

_____

_____

Taste

I emcee the World Culinary Showcase at the National Restaurant Show in Chicago, and almost every celebrity chef on the stage tells a story of how being in the kitchen at a young age with their mother or grandmother inspired them to become chefs. Taste is always central to their stories.

I am not a chef, but the taste of Lawry's seasoned salt literally puts me right back in the kitchen with my nana, who sprinkled it on the perfectly poached eggs she made for me every morning when I slept over. The memory makes me try a little harder in my own kitchen, even though I now use a salt substitute because I'm no longer twelve. But I definitely sprinkle Lawry's on my kids' eggs because I love my nana.

What tastes remind you of your career or a career you desire?

_____

_____

_____

Pay attention to what pleases your five senses. There is a reason why the smells, tastes, sounds, feels, and sights please you. They are your five main tools for how you perceive the world. They are your home and can guide you to your story, your purpose, and your career. They are the ministers to your soul.

Don't forget about your sixth sense. It may not be one of the five, but it is definitely my favorite and the most powerful. Your sixth sense becomes highly tuned when you tap into it, and it should never be ignored. It is literally the rudder that guides you always. Listening to our own voice unlocks the power and potential we have as speakers and humans. Unlock your sixth sense, and use it as you move through life.

If you want to raise all five of your senses (and your sixth) to the next level, never hold back on giving a compliment to someone. Compliments are the best way to connect with people, and they usually please all five of our senses—both those of the receiver of the compliment as well as those of the giver.

When I launched my business lovespeaks, I attended my first networking event. I have no fear entering a room with thousands of people, a microphone, and a purpose. But entering a room of a hundred professional women I didn't know and without a purpose terrified me.

As I was riding up in the elevator, a woman said to me, "I love your outfit." That's all it took to quiet my fear. Her name is Alyssa Burns, and she was my go-to-girl for my first networking event because she gave me a compliment. Alyssa is still one of my favorite friends, and I will always be grateful to her for making my first networking moment easy by simply giving me a compliment.

Forbes reports that there is scientific proof that when we receive a compliment for our talent, it feels as good as receiving a cash reward. Make compliments your currency. Give them, and receive them. Use compliments like cash. Don't save them. They don't work like paper currency. They have no value when they are saved. They only have value when they are shared. Compliments connect us just like our stories.

I was on a flight when an enormous man sat down next to me. When I say enormous, I mean the muscles in his arms and legs were so big (and chiseled) that I could barely move when he sat down. His right bicep was basically in my face. But he smelled so good. Once he got himself settled into his seat, it was obvious I was uncomfortable.

And that's when I looked at him and said, "Excuse me, but can I just say that you smell so good!" It was totally unexpected, and the smile on his face made me so happy that I forgot I hated to fly. Air travel is hard enough, and if you've bothered to shower and smell delicious, you should be complimented, even if your bicep is in someone else's face. Compliments change everything.

I will never forget when a producer from a big brand I was speaking for came up to me after my keynote and said, "You know what I like about you, Sally Lou?" I said, "No, what?" He said, "You're not slick." I didn't know whether to take his comment as a complete insult or as a compliment.

But as I sat with his words for a few moments, I realized it was a total compliment. I am not slick, and that is what makes me talented. People who authentically connect with others are not always so slick.

Whatever your talent is, the unique thing that makes you who you are, own it, and make it yours. I use my "unslick" and unexpected doling out of compliments in every part of my life, whether I'm on a stage, on a plane, on a street, or in Starbucks. The power of how we can shift the energy around us is very cool.

And by all means, if you are on an interview for a job that you really want, compliment the person who is taking the time to speak to you if you really want an offer.

LOVESPEAKS LESSON #4: Pay attention to environments that suck you in and please all five of your senses. Spend time there. That is your home. When you use your talent in an environment you love, it never feels like work.

What is your most highly developed sense?

_____

_____

_____

LOVESPEAKS PRACTICE: Notice a smell, a sound, a taste, a sight, and a feeling that pleases you. Write down what sense speaks to you the most. Review the senses that please you and see if you are incorporating them into your life professionally or personally. If you aren't, find a way to do so.

ALTERNATIVE LOVESPEAKS PRACTICE: If you are not in tune with your senses, take time to develop them. Literally stop and smell the roses. Eat a meal more slowly and savor the taste. Try something you have never eaten before. Listen for sounds in nature that bring calm to your day. Keep things close to you that make you feel comfortable. I bring my clipboard with me every time I speak and my cashmere blanket every time I fly.

See the beauty that surrounds you every day of your life. Take photographs of beautiful things, and start a folder in your phone just for you. Check in with your photos when you need a reminder. Or go outside and look for more beauty.

LIVE LOVESPEAKS: Meet Whitney. My friend Whitney Reynolds, mom of twins and host and owner of *The Whitney Reynolds Show*, aired on several PBS markets, starts her story with "a girl with a dream turned woman on a mission." As a young girl, Whitney used to interview her dolls in her bedroom and pretend to be a talk show host.

She decided at a very young age that she would be a broadcaster and was determined to use her talent in an environment she loved, a TV studio. In 2009 when we produced the flash mob dance on Michigan Avenue with The Black Eyed Peas, I was on the stage warming up the audience of twenty-three thousand people while famed director Michael Gracey taught the audience the dance.

Out of the crowd, I heard a young woman with a distinct Southern drawl scream "Hey! I am gonna to be the next Oprah Winfrey!" I remember looking at her and saying, "Yes, you are!" That was twenty-three-year-old Whitney Reynolds, speaking her story and about to make it happen. I didn't know Whitney then, but I believed her.

Today the Emmy-nominated talk show host is dedicated to provoking positive change through tough topics on her talk show that she hosts and owns. That sure sounds like Oprah to me! Whitney also hosts inspiring segments on iHeartRadio and is a columnist for *Chicago Parent Magazine*, where she uses her voice for change.

Whitney reminds us that our words have power and that if we have talents that we want to use in an environment that pleases all five of our senses, all we have to do is announce our goals to a crowd of twenty-three thousand people and watch it happen. We can also announce our dream to just one person. That works too.

My talent when I was young
was _____.

The environment I
love is _____.

The sense that pleases me the most in the
environment I love is _____
because it_____.

My career
today is _____.

Or I want a
career in _____.

CHAPTER 5

Don't Tilt the Boxes

I'd like to be remembered as someone who did the best she could with the talent she had.

—J. K. ROWLING

Like many of us, my childhood set the stage for the human I am today and the career path I chose. Everything I ever needed to know was in a box my grandmother delivers at the end of this chapter. Stick with me!

My family calls me Lulu or Loulie or Sally Lou. Never Sally. That's reserved for Denzel. I identify with Lulu the most. When someone calls me Sally, I immediately know they don't know me or don't want to take the time to know me.

Every time I meet new people and they say, "It's nice to meet you, Sally Lou," I always say, "Thanks for the Lou!" It makes me feel so happy when someone takes the time to say my entire name. When you have a difficult name, you develop a great love for others who do as well. And if you have a double name, you are automatically my friend. The collection of names I get on my Starbucks cups is endless. My favorite is Sally Woo, and no, I am not from Whoville. I'm not even from the South.

My name is a lot to explain. Most people don't get that I have two first names. My great-grandmother's name was Sarah Louise, and everyone called her Sally Lou. My grandmother loved her grandmother, so she named her daughter Sally Lou, and my parents loved my aunt, so they named me Sally Lou. My sister Cindy named one of her daughters Sarah Louise, but everyone calls her Lucy because our family likes to make names difficult.

My grandmother, who started the "Sally Lou" tradition, was the one who made tea sandwiches. Her name was Marion, and we called her Mom Mom. My other grandparents, Pop Pop and Nana, were named Joseph and

Marian. Both my grandmothers shared the same name with a different spelling, giving my husband and I a great reason to name our daughter Marin. I couldn't make a choice on which way to spell the name, so we dropped the last vowel and settled on Marin.

All three of my grandparents were huge influences in my life. On any given Saturday, you could find me at one of their two homes. I am the baby of three girls, and my two older sisters, who are only two years apart, did a lot together. I was "the baby," and they were "the girls." I played the role of baby all day long and still do. My dad also called me Tiny Tank or Tanker, which pretty much made it impossible for me to ever live up to "the girls."

If Tanker wasn't bad enough, I also wore a brace on my legs when I was little because I walked like a duck. Every night before I went to bed, my mom would strap on the brace that had two shoes on either end to straighten my feet. That's how I slept.

My sisters thought it was pretty funny, and before bedtime they would put me on the middle of my twin bed and bounce me on either side, causing me to lose my balance and fall off the bed. They'd pick me up, put me back on the bed, and continue to jump again. They thought it was hilarious, and I just thought it was my role as "the baby." I existed for their pleasure.

Prior to the bed-bouncing torment, my sister Susan actually saved my life. I was probably four years old, and I was wearing my snowsuit, which I could barely move in, when my mom put me in the back seat of our station wagon along with my sisters and drove up our long driveway.

When my mom turned onto our busy street, I fell out of the car and into a snowbank on the street. (I must have been leaning against the door.) I wasn't wearing a seat belt either. This was before the seat belt law. I'm not even sure our Oldsmobile had seat belts. Susan screamed, "Mom, stop the car. Loulie fell out!" So my mom stopped the car, and Susan pulled me back in. I guess I hadn't closed the door properly, and no one else had bothered to check.

As I got older, I hated being in the car because it meant that my mom was driving the girls to a sporting event in swimming, gymnastics, field hockey, or lacrosse and that I had to go too. The worst was swimming. I would have to sit in the stands for what seemed like an eternity. To this day, the smell of an indoor pool gives me immediate anxiety.

I was an athlete too, but not like my sisters. I preferred hanging out with my grandparents and listening to their stories. So I opted to spend Saturdays at one of their houses instead of spending it all day in the back of my mom's station wagon or worse, inside an indoor pool.

My mom's parents were my fancy grandparents. My nana was always dressed impeccably, and her nails were meticulously manicured. She kept her *gifts with purchase* that she received from the Saks Fifth Avenue makeup counter in her bathroom closet, and whenever I spent the night, I went home with one.

Every night at exactly five thirty, my nana prepared dinner for my grandfather, starting with an array of carrots, celery, radishes, and black olives served over a bed of ice along with two shot glasses for their two allotted cocktails. They drank Canadian club on the rocks. My nana stuck to her allotment, but I'm pretty sure my grandfather did not.

Pop Pop had a great sense of humor and was always playing practical jokes, which is where my mom gets her humor. He told us his cousin ran away with the circus, and since Pop Pop's last name was Skelton, we all believed the comic character Red Skelton was our cousin. Red Skelton was a famous comic, so I'd like to think we are related. Being the full baby that I was, I fell for all my grandfather's jokes.

Evidently, so did everyone else. When my mother was born, my grandfather walked into my nana's hospital room and said, "Well, look who it is, little baby Snooks," when he saw my mother. Fanny Brice was the star of *The Baby Snooks Show*, and she was not attractive, so my grandfather thought his nickname for my mom was hilarious.

Later, Barbra Streisand, who was a goddess in our house and still is, played Fanny Brice in *Funny Girl* on Broadway, so basically, we are related to Barbra Streisand too. From the day she was born, my mother, whose name is Mary Ann, was called Snookie.

Growing up, my mom spent every summer in Ocean City, New Jersey, with her grandparents because her grandfather taught tennis at the Ocean City Tennis Club, making her the original Snookie of the Jersey Shore. My mom spells her name with an E at the end, one of the many differences the two Snooki/Snookies have.

Having sold his oil business, JJ Skelton & Son, to Gulf Oil at fifty-four, my grandfather retired early. His father started the business as a coal yard and my grandfather, with only a high school degree, built the business into something he would eventually sell. Since my grandfather had time on his hands, he chose to hang out with me on most Saturdays while he landscaped his yard, which was so meticulously kept that it rivaled my grandmother's manicure.

I had no idea what retired meant at ten years old because my father was always at work. But I definitely thought my grandfather was a landscaper since he was always working in his yard. Landscaping was his talent, and he practiced that talent every weekend I visited.

Pop Pop was big in stature and personality and was always dressed in a pair of pressed khaki pants and a crisp button-down shirt with a light zip-up jacket. All his business suits hung in his closet and were labeled in individual suit bags. His garage smelled like fresh cement, new cars, and wood. It was so clean that we could have eaten my nana's homemade dinners right off the floor.

Whenever I get a whiff of that combination of cement, new cars, and wood, I always think of my pop pop, and it makes me happy. It also reminds me to clean my own garage, which even at its most organized, would never live up to his. My garage is basically an overstocked puzzle. Everything fits neatly together, but there is way too much stuff. My grandfather would not approve.

When he wasn't driving his pristine Lincoln Continental, my grandfather was riding his lawn mower to cut the grass. He worked hard while I enjoyed rolling down the hill, covered in freshly cut grass by the time I reached the bottom. My pop pop took great pleasure in making everything look perfect, which may be where I get my love for things fitting neatly together. It's also possible he is the reason I love shopping since his closet looked and smelled like Bergdorf Goodman, but I blame my mom.

On both sides of my grandfather's perfectly landscaped lawn stood two magnificent terra-cotta urns. The terra-cotta urns were huge, and the bigger of the two served as home base for my neighborhood games. I spent so much time at my grandparents' house that I made friends in their neighborhood. Red light green light, hide-and-go-seek, and kick the can were our go-to games.

When it was time to start hide-and-go-seek, I would put my head into the home-base terra-cotta urn and scream, "Ready or not, here I come!" My small voice filled the big urn, and I could feel its power. It was like I had plugged myself into an amplifier. Then off I would go to find my friends with a powerful sense of excitement.

Whenever it stormed, my grandfather and I would sit under his awning-covered porch and watch the rain while my grandmother made dinner inside in her perfect outfit. I was scared of the thunder and lightning—and I still am—but sitting by my grandfather made me feel safe, even though he teased me relentlessly with every crack of lightning.

My grandfather was always looking for the joke. I remember being confused as to how an older aunt of ours was related to us, and I asked him, "Pop Pop, who is Aunt Bibi to you?"

And he answered, "A pain in the ass!" His timing was perfect.

Anytime he drove me anywhere, Pop Pop would pretend we were lost and laugh. I would pretend to laugh too, but honestly, I was legitimately terrified we were lost, which is probably why my husband makes me maps whenever I need to drive somewhere I'm not familiar with. I just don't trust GPS, and I definitely don't trust myself. Having a sense of direction is not one of my talents, but fashion definitely is.

I come from a long line of fashionistas. My nana's mother owned a children's dress boutique and my nana's style was impeccable. When my nana died at age eighty-five, we found a page in her wallet that she had torn out of the Saks catalog of a purple Louis Féraud suit that she was planning to buy.

My nana was always the best dressed women in the room, and she wasn't going to let age stop her from exercising her talent. My mom dressed her in her favorite Frank Agostino suit and put a beautiful lace handkerchief in her hand when she was laid to rest. Marian Marshall Skelton left this world exactly how she lived in this world—with magnificent style.

Once when we took *The Oprah Winfrey Show* to New York City, my mom was sitting in the audience, and Ivana Trump (not Ivanka), who was a guest on the show, picked her out of the crowd as the most fashionable woman. Like all fashion icons, my mom stood up and gave a wave to her fans.

When I was ten years old, my mom invited me to go on an errand with her to our local pharmacy, the Gladwyne Pharmacy, which was basically the center of my world because it was stocked with candy and we had a house charge. I liked that everyone knew me there because I was one of the Oaks girls.

When we walked in, my mom said hello to her friend Lizanne, who was standing at the register with her sister. Lizanne introduced my mom to her sister, who was a magnificent woman wearing a simple caftan shirt, lightweight summer pants, and her hair was wrapped in a turban.

After the two women left, my mom turned to the cashier and said, "You just rang up Princess Grace of Monaco's purchases." The cashier was shocked, and so was I. Grace Kelly was born in Philadelphia at Hahnemann Hospital to a prominent Philadelphia family, and her sister Lizanne lived around the corner from us in Gladwyne. Grace Kelly was a beautiful woman from Philadelphia who grew up to be a princess. My mom is a beautiful woman from Philadelphia who grew up to be my mom.

My mom is thirty years older than me, and I don't even like taking photos with her. First of all, she has this incredible pose that I don't have. Second, she dresses impeccably just like my nana did and kills it every time. Third, she is photogenic, and one of the few eighty-seven-year-olds who prefers high heels and sends selfies. My mom isn't a princess, but she is my queen.

I was recognized for my fashion talent when I was booked as a guest on *The Oprah Winfrey Show* in 1987 for wearing cute outfits. When I got on the stage, I was told the show was titled *Shopaholics.*

There I was sitting next to Zsa Zsa Gabor, a celebrity who was known for her outlandish spending and crazy outfits, outed on national television as a shopaholic. The producers told me that they just wanted to show some footage of my closet because I came to work wearing a cute outfit every day. Next thing you know I am on the stage telling my boss, Oprah Winfrey, that I have a psychological disorder. That's not exactly the best way to impress your boss.

I will say my haircut caught a lot of attention, and our phone lines lit up with people calling to ask where they could go to get the same style. My hairdresser, Irene, got a lot of new clients, and I got a nice price for my future haircuts.

I wore a fabulous gold belt with hanging charms designed by jewelry designer Linda Levinson, and Oprah mentioned that she had the same belt too, which was when it dawned on me that I had made a large mistake. If I remember correctly, the boutique where I had purchased the belt sold about twenty-five belts that day, and they weren't cheap. No one knew what an influencer was back then, but I was one for a brief moment.

The same year as my *Oprah Winfrey Show* debut, my husband, who was my boyfriend at the time, invited me to a fancy party his parents were hosting. This is shocking news, but I had nothing to wear! My seventh-grade girlfriend BJ Nipon, one of my groovy friends who wore cliffy low-cuts and huckapoo shirts, shipped her mother's dress to me to wear.

BJ's parents, Albert and Pearl Nipon, were fashion designers, and her mother, Pearl, was a style icon. As a teenager, I used to visit their dress factory in Philadelphia with my mom and sometimes with BJ. Pearl was the first woman I had ever known who ran a company, and she made an enormous impact on me. Wearing Pearl Nipon's dress and a pair of earrings I'd borrowed from my boss Fran, off I went to impress my future in-laws, dressed in nothing I owned.

At the party, I was dancing with my husband's best friend, Peter Cristal, and my earrings kept falling off. I told Peter to stay right where he was and that I would be right back to finish our dance. I ran into the house at top speed to safely store my boss's earrings and didn't notice that the screen door was pulled shut. It was dark, and I didn't want to miss one more second of my dance with Peter, so unknowingly, I ran into a closed screen door and took that screen door down with my body in my Albert Nipon dress and my boss's earrings.

Springs and nails went flying through the air, and I rode that screen door into the house like a surfboard. Needless to say that I missed the rest of my dance with Peter and was totally embarrassed, but I kept my fashion game strong.

My grandmother Mom Mom was not fancy. She wasn't a shopaholic or a fashion icon either. I'm pretty certain she never owned a designer dress. She was the tea sandwich maker, and she lost her husband to cancer when she was forty-six years old and he was fifty-one. It was 1950, and as a young widow, my mom mom was left to raise her fourteen-year-old son, Jody, on her own.

My uncle Jody was born premature with cerebral palsy and intellectual disabilities. For as long as I knew Jody, he was in a wheelchair. My father and his sister, my aunt Sally Lou, whom I adored, were already out of the house when they lost their father, so my grandmother was left to raise Jody on her own, even though my dad and aunt helped her as much as they could.

Before having my dad, my aunt Sally Lou, and my uncle Jody, Mom Mom lost two baby girls, Elizabeth and June, to tuberculosis. After losing her husband and two babies, there was no way my strong-willed and loving grandmother, the mighty Marion, would allow Jody to be placed in a home to be cared for. She had already lost so much.

The Oaks family is not built that way. So Mom Mom figured out a way to earn a living without ever having to leave her house, except when she drove to the Penn Fruit for groceries, and that was a big event. She would fire up her green Chevy Nova after putting Jody in the car and his wheelchair in the trunk, and off they would go to buy groceries. I literally don't know how she did it.

Mrs. Oaks's Tea Sandwiches was born from my grandmother's need to stay home with Jody and earn a living. Luckily, because Mom Mom put her talent to work, she quickly became known for her delicious works of art. If I had been old enough, I would have helped her build her brand with a cute logo, but none of us thought like that back then. She would have had a killer Instagram account today.

There was a process to my grandmother's tea sandwich making and that process included a community of women. Every day my grandmother's dining room table was filled with women of all ages. They gathered at Mrs. Oaks's house to make tea sandwiches. Some rolled the bread, some cut the crust, some spread the inside filling, and some decorated.

The decorators were in a league of their own. I wanted to be decorator so badly, but I never got past crust-cutting and spreading. Of course, my sister Susan, who can pretty much do anything she sets her mind to, was an excellent decorator. Cindy ate the crust out of the discard bag, and I waited for the customers to arrive. Cindy was the only one out of character because she has absolutely zero body fat and I have never seen her eat a piece of bread since.

Sandwich making was why the women assembled at my grandmother's table, but there was so much more going on at that table than the work. The community of women who gathered at that table each day helped my grandmother raise Jody. As he sat in his wheelchair at the table, the women would tend to Jody all day long while supporting my grandmother's business.

It was the most beautiful community to watch. My tiny little grandmother, all of about four feet eleven inches, would instruct the ladies on what to do while tending to her son, always with a cream cheese-loaded decorating gun in her hand. It was the happiest table I have ever seen. It was a community that worked.

The cool thing about my grandmother was she allowed Jody to be a man as he got older. She let him smoke a pipe and drink a glass of vodka sometimes while he watched his beloved Philadelphia Phillies baseball team. I think one of my first lessons in seeing love speak was experiencing Jody watch Hall of Fame third-basemen Mike Schmidt play baseball. Mike Schmidt made Jody's face light up like a scoreboard.

Because my grandmother didn't get much sleep and there was always a lot going on at her table, she would get mixed up sometimes. One afternoon she gave Mrs. Endy, an elderly woman who was a frequent visitor at the table and also in a wheelchair, Jody's pipe and gave Jody Mrs. Endy's medicine. Jody and Mrs. Endy both had a look of shock on their faces that to this day makes me and my family laugh so hard.

Whenever we have a mix-up in our family, which is often, we say, "Mom, where's my pipe?" I had a near miss when I almost mixed up our dog Tinker's morning dose of Viagra with Billy's morning dose of ADHD medicine. Viagra was keeping Tinker's heart pumping, and the ADHD meds were keeping Billy focused. Both pills looked exactly the same, and I was seconds away from a very large mix-up. Thank God I wasn't the mom who sent her fifteen-year-old son off to high school with a dose of Viagra because he would have really lost his focus.

I always wanted a brother, and Jody fulfilled that wish for me. I loved teaching him new things like the alphabet or colors. Sometimes I helped my grandmother exercise Jody on his parallel bars, but most of all, I just loved him. I threw my arms around him and kissed him all over his face. I talked to him nonstop, and I loved watching his heart explode with joy.

But being the scaredy-cat kid that I was, Jody also scared me sometimes because he was a choker. My grandmother crushed his medicine and gave it to him in orange juice, which is why I was eighteen when I finally learned how to swallow a pill.

When I was five, I stopped swallowing food altogether. I chewed my food and kept it in my cheeks. When I was at my nana's house, she would discreetly hold a paper napkin in her manicured hand for me to spit my food into and quietly dispose of it. I thought if I swallowed my food, I would choke like Jody.

When I was at Mom Mom's house and Jody choked at dinner, I ran out of the room and hid in the closet and covered my ears while my sister Susan gave Jody the Heimlich maneuver. Susan became a physician's assistant, and I did not. Clearly, I learned to swallow food, but I always tell my kids that I have a "no choking" rule and that they'd better abide by it.

Jody had one story to tell, and every time he told it, we would cheer and smile and hug him. We asked him where he lived, and he always had the answer. "In Wynnewood," he would scream. That was Jody's story. He lived in Wynnewood, Pennsylvania, and he told it beautifully. Later my grandmother and Jody moved to Cape May Court House, New Jersey, to be closer to my aunt Sally Lou, but he still told his Wynnewood story with all his heart.

Every time my dad entered the room, Jody would literally burst into tears. He loved my dad so much that the joy of seeing him made Jody cry. Jody and my dad shared a bed growing up because my grandmother was famous for taking in family members who needed help. So my dad gave up his room and never had a bed of his own until he went to college.

The problem with sharing a bed was that Jody wore braces to bed, and his braces were big. Jody's twin bed and braces left little room for my dad, but my dad never complained because Jody was the heart of his family. Luckily, my dad was also a little guy.

Jody lived to be forty-five years old, and I dream about him all the time. I can feel his heart through my dreams so strongly just like I felt when I was kissing his face. He is the reason why my grandmother started her tea sandwich business, and it was the business that allowed for a community of women to connect every day at my grandmother's dining room table. This community of women helped my grandmother make tea sandwiches, but it was Jody who kept them coming back day after day.

Whenever a customer arrived to pick up their sandwiches, my grandmother would carefully bring their order to the door and say in her sweet voice, "Don't tilt the boxes," as they left. Those tea sandwiches were her babies, and nobody messed with my grandmother's babies. The idea of any food colored cream cheese icing touching the top of the box or sliding in any way made her crazy. Tilting was not an option.

My grandmother's tea sandwiches were made with love, and that love was carried to other family's tables. Her customers delighted in displaying and eating her sandwiches and felt love from the community of women and Jody in every bite. We all know that food always tastes better when it's made with love.

There is no question that Mom Mom inspired me to love my talent and was my inspiration to start my own business. I may not make pretty tea sandwiches, but my hope is that the community I have created through my business feels as much love when they see me on a stage, at an event, on Facebook, on Instagram, or in their in-box as my grandmother's customers felt when they arrived at her door.

I would never tilt the box on my talent. Whatever your talent is, don't ever tilt the box on yours. We have each been blessed with something to give the world. My grandmother made sandwiches. I connect with people. You may design skyscrapers or wedding gowns or drive for Uber. Whatever it is you do well, whether you are being paid for it or not, protect it with your life the way my grandmother protected her talent.

LOVESPEAKS LESSON #5: Connect with your audience by caring for your craft, and build your community by doing what you love. Don't ever tilt the box on whatever beautiful talent you have been blessed with. Nurture it. Love it. Share it with others.

We can't be successful alone. We need a community of people to lean on in good times and bad. We need people to share their talents with us and we need to share our talents with them. Having a community that is committed to our personal progress is a gift. Whether you are a crust cutter, a spreader, or a decorator, your talent is key to your community.

We can travel the world and always know that even if our community isn't sitting at our table, they are always an email, FaceTime, Skype, text, or Starbucks away.

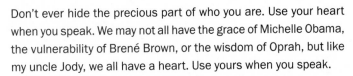

SPEAK

Don't ever hide the precious part of who you are. Use your heart when you speak. We may not all have the grace of Michelle Obama, the vulnerability of Brené Brown, or the wisdom of Oprah, but like my uncle Jody, we all have a heart. Use yours when you speak.

Who in your community reminds you to use your heart when you speak?

_____

_____

_____

LOVESPEAKS PRACTICE: Tell yourself daily that we are better together than we are apart. Reach out to someone in your circle who has talents you don't have. The team you have built or are building right now—the team that doesn't look like you, act like you, think like you, or share the same talents you have—is the team that will take you where you want to go.

Begin sharing your talents with others and ask others to share their talents with you. When you see people who have talents you don't have, invite them into your world and share your talents with one another.

ALTERNATIVE LOVESPEAKS PRACTICE: Whatever it is you feel is your weakness, write it down, and claim it. Spend some time visualizing yourself developing that weakness into a strength. See the people who have the strength you want coming into your life. Speak this wish into the universe.

One day you will unexpectedly be blessed with someone who was sent to you to do just that, namely help you develop your weakness into a strength. When that someone arrives, invite them into your life.

LIVE LOVESPEAKS: Meet Mona. My friend Mona Antwan is a mother of two and founder of Mindfulness Leader, a not-for-profit dedicated to transforming the city of Chicago's youth. Mona has been practicing mindfulness for nineteen years, and she starts her story with "empowering the youth to lead from within."

I met Mona at Harpo where she worked as an accountant. I was drawn to her immediately because she loves saving money as much as I love spending it. Her mindfulness around money was something I could benefit from and a talent I didn't have. We instantly became friends.

After *The Oprah Winfrey Show* ended, Mona shared with me that she wanted to start a mindfulness program for students in Chicago. Having started my own LLC, I was happy to help her with any advice.

Mona has a powerful story. She emigrated from Baghdad, Iraq, in 1980 with her parents and siblings. She told me that not knowing the language and adjusting to a whole new culture was extremely difficult at six years old.

By the third grade, Mona was speaking English fluently and advocating for all the other kids from other countries who were not catching up with the language as quickly as she was. That's when she knew that being an unseen and unheard child was preparing her for a lifetime of service, and Mona made a choice to lead from within.

Mindfulness Leader is an innovative project-based course with twenty-three core principles that include valuable life skills such as developing personal confidence. Students get direct access to resources that bring balance to their lives and the power to be the best versions of themselves.

Mona's program has been recognized by the White House, and she was recently invited to Nigeria to train students, teachers, and parents on mindfulness. My prayer is that Mindfulness Leader will be a program offered across the country to make lasting changes in the lives of our youth.

Mona, whom I call Money, is part of my community and my team. We don't look like each other, we don't think like each other, and we don't have the same talents. But we both benefit from each other, which is why Mona is on my team.

You don't have to work for the same company or share an office with people for them to be on your team. You can have anyone you want on your team. You know why? Because it's *your* team!

Who is on your team?

_____

_____

_____

CHAPTER 6

From Mighty Oaks Little Acorns Grow

We rise by lifting others.
—ROBERT INGERSOLL

My dad gave me my heart, and he is my speaker hero number four. There is never a moment in my life when I don't recognize and give thanks for the great privilege it was to be my father's daughter. I could have been born to another set of parents, but God chose mine. I am forever grateful, and as you read the stories in this chapter, you will understand my career did not happen by accident.

My dad was just like his mother, Mom Mom, except his talent was medicine, not tea sandwiches. His father was a doctor, and when my dad was a young boy, he accompanied his father on many house calls, which sparked a love of medicine in my dad. When my dad became a doctor, he also became a workaholic. My dad never turned work off. He was always ready to save someone's life. He wasn't perfect, but he was Superman to me.

When my dad wasn't seeing patients or teaching at Hahnemann Hospital (where Princess Grace was born), he was serving at St. John's Hospice homeless clinic, mentoring student athletes at his alma mater, Lafayette College, catching one of our field hockey or lacrosse games, speaking at a medical conference, stopping by a church to say a quick prayer, or driving to the Jersey Shore to see his mom, his brother, and his sister. He also managed to fit some time in for my mom too. They had a beautiful marriage and they were great partners and role models to me and my sisters. It wasn't perfect because my father worked too much, but whose marriage is?

My dad never left home without his stethoscope, and whenever he saw anyone along his way who needed saving, he was ready to serve. And yet he managed to spend more time with his three daughters than most nine-to-five working fathers did. I'm not sure how he did it, but he was the son of the Mighty Marion, and he was always there for us for anything we needed. And wherever he was needed, he always managed to get there fast just like Superman.

Mom Mom called my dad B. I always thought B was for Billy, but I learned later that her nickname for him was actually Bee, not B, because she said he was as *busy as a bee*. That was my dad—a whirling dervish of love and speed.

That airplane we almost died in was my dad's way of getting to me fast. He chartered a small plane to pick me up in Nantucket, where I was on vacation with Betsy and my other best friend Kelsey. On the day we were leaving, I woke up with severe abdominal pain and was taken to the Nantucket Cottage Hospital. My dad did not like the word *cottage*, so he chartered a plane to get me because Nantucket is an island and hard to get to. Private air travel was not exactly in our family's budget. In fact commercial air travel wasn't in our family's budget. But my dad was not normal.

He had the biggest heart a human could possibly have, and he was also a huge worrier, so my dad chartered a plane to save me because that is what Dr. Oaks does. He saves lives. My dad always told us, "It will all be okay," but underneath that message was also one of worry. I struggle with worry too. In fact, you could call me a professional worrier, which is why I am dedicated to my meditation and prayer practice, the only thing that quiets my worry.

My dad never smoked cigarettes or drank alcohol because he knew those things would get in the way of him being an all-American athlete. And even though my dad was not an all-American athlete, he was always striving to be one, and that was all that mattered.

When he got home after working a seventeen-hour day, my dad would run the hill of our street several times to stay in shape. He raised my sisters and me to be athletes because being a part of a team was integral to my father's life, and he wanted to make sure it was at the center of ours. We played a sport every season, beginning in grade school, and we were in training all year. There was no off season for the Oaks girls or Dr. Oaks. We were either in preseason or in the season. We were always working hard to be the best we could be—a mantra my dad instilled in us from an early age.

Years later Lafayette College named their men's soccer stadium Oaks Stadium after my dad, not because he was a huge donor but because he was a huge lover and supporter of the team. You could always find my dad standing on the thirteenth step that led to the field near the stadium entrance, watching a soccer game.

Thirteen was my dad's medical number and his lucky number, and the number three was his soccer jersey when he played at Lafayette. My dad was very superstitious, and numbers were important to him. Three and thirteen were his favorites, and both numbers show up now in my own life a lot, probably because I am looking for them.

When my dad turned eighty, we made Team Oaksie soccer jerseys in maroon and white, Lafayette College's school colors, and we chartered a bus to take the Oaks team to Oaks Stadium and to celebrate my dad at a soccer game. We sang cheers the whole way up to campus, and my dad never sat down on the bus ride because he was as *busy as a bee*, talking and singing with his team. My dad had a beautiful voice and was always looking for an opportunity to harmonize. We were always prepared to sing our part, but he always made us sound better.

The soccer team dedicated the game to my dad that day, and I can't remember if they won, but I remember the heartfelt birthday toast the team made after the game, and it was clear how beloved my dad was to the program. My sisters and I all played sports on the fields next to Oaks Stadium as did a few of my dad's granddaughters, so this was my dad's happy place.

My daughter Carly, who attended Lafayette College, made the fields at Oaks Stadium her own as a camera operator and director of the online feed of the soccer games, which I thought was just about the coolest way to combine everything the Loveman as well as the Oaks families loved. Being on a field, watching a team play any sport, especially soccer, and having the Oaks team beside him were the three things my dad loved the most, besides medicine, which was always number one.

When I was training for the Presidential Physical Fitness Award in fifth grade, I brought home a softball and measuring tape every weekend so my dad could teach me how to throw the ball fifty feet. I didn't get the award until sixth grade because I couldn't complete the required fifty sit-ups, even though I somehow managed to throw the ball fifty feet. I was on sit-up number forty-nine and had a good ten seconds left to get that last sit-up, and I literally couldn't complete it.

But I was in training, and that was all that mattered. Mr. Di Battista, my grammar school gym teacher, taught me and my sisters to appreciate being physically fit. Every time I run, do a push-up, a sit up or a squat jump, I think of Mr. DB and how grateful I am that he taught me the importance of exercising with good form.

Being on Mr. DB's safety patrol was as close as I would ever get to feeling like I was in a dance competition. When I watch Beyoncé's *Homecoming* performance at Coachella, I kind of see some of our safety patrol moves and wish I had stuck with it.

But I can throw a football. Susan and Cindy can throw one way better than me, but I can send one spiraling! We spent a lot of time throwing and catching footballs every summer on the Jersey Shore, and my dad gave us each a football jersey of our own to wear when we played, which called for more nicknames. Nicknames were my father's way of letting you know you mattered to him. So if you knew my dad, you had a nickname.

When we were little, my dad used to tell us the story of *Goldilocks and the Three Bears* before we went to bed. Only his three bears were Mike Ditka, Gayle Sayers, and Sid Luckman preparing me for a city he and I had no idea I would one day call home. These guys were my dad's three favorite Chicago Bears.

Every once in a while, I would go to the hospital on the weekends with my dad when he made rounds with his patients. We would walk the halls of the hospital, and everyone would say, "Dr. Oaks! Dr. Oaks!" I felt like I was traveling with a rock star, and I liked it. It felt good to be part of something bigger than myself.

He knew everyone by name, and of course, they usually had nicknames. He said hello to every single person who passed us by, from the doctors to the custodial staff. My dad believed that everyone mattered and everyone played a role in the success of the hospital. This was his team. My dad was my Oprah before Oprah was my Oprah, making it very clear why the universe led me to Oprah.

My dad had a unique ability of making everyone believe they were his favorite person. In fact, my sisters and I had an argument over the fact that we each believed we were his favorite. When someone asked who our mom's favorite was, I said, "I'm not!" Susan said, "I'm not." Cindy said, "I'm not!" That pretty much sums up my parents. (Love you, Mom!)

My visits to the hospital helped me discover that I wanted to be part of the magic I felt when I was with my dad. I wanted to help people. I wanted to impact people's lives. I wanted to ride with a rock star. But I knew I wasn't doctor material, and the hospital environment did not please all five of my senses. I loved the feel of the camaraderie of the team, but that's where it ended.

It was hard for my dad's team to keep up with him because my dad was always in training and never took the elevator. It wasn't because he was scared of them like I am but because he wanted to stay in shape. So if you were an attending, a medical student, or an intern and you needed to talk to my dad, you were taking the stairs too. The hospital had sixteen floors, which is I guess why my dad was only 138 pounds, my goal weight.

He also never drove a car that wasn't a convertible, which fit his eternally young personality completely. I'm pretty sure my dad was one of the first wave of people to ever have a car phone. That's what we called them in the 1970s—car phones. It was a big phone that was installed into his car, and it was really clunky.

It had about twenty huge buttons on the frame of the phone that lit up like an operator's switchboard. In order to get a free line, you had to click on a button and see if the line was available. Which meant that when you clicked on a line that wasn't available, you could hear an entire conversation between strangers.

My dad had the phone because he always wanted to be able to be reached. His phone gave him access to anyone who needed saving. It also allowed him to call us just before he pulled out of the hospital's parking lot to head home. Every night my dad would call to say, "I'm on my way," which were the four most treasured words of my childhood.

"I'm on my way" meant my dad would be home, the house would be safe, and I could sleep knowing he was up watching a game on TV, dictating his medical notes, eating a late dinner with my mom, or reading the newspaper. I learned to sleep in a noisy house, which is why I don't love the quiet.

My dad never said goodbye before he hung up the phone. I'm not even sure he said goodbye in person. It's like the word was never an option for my dad, but he loved his car phone and he used it to help save lives.

In the rare moments my dad was home from work, I would sneak into the garage, punch the buttons on his car phone, and listen in on conversations. I know it sounds totally wrong, and it was, but I couldn't stop listening. I wanted to hear the stories. My parents caught on and cut me off.

I remember saying to them, "I hope one day we will have picture phones." Every time I FaceTime my kids, I think about that moment in my garage at 914 Stony Lane, which we called The Five Oaks because we were a family of five and our house had five oak trees in the front lawn, and I say, "Wow. Who knew?"

Growing up, I loved my dad's friends. They were known as the Cynwyd Clowns (the C is pronounced like a K) because they grew up in Bala Cynwyd, Pennsylvania. My uncle Bill McCarter and my uncle Price Norris lived on our street when we lived on Black Rock Road before we moved to our house on Stony Lane. They weren't uncles by blood, but they were Cynwyd Clowns, which made them family.

My uncle Scotty, another Cynwyd Clown, lived a few streets away and was married to my mom's best friend, my aunt Mary, who introduced my mom and dad on July 22, 1950, in Ocean City, New Jersey. If anyone, including my dad, messed with Uncle Price, Uncle Bill, or Uncle Scotty, they had to deal with me.

The Cynwyd Clowns had a slogan: "First in peace. First in war. Cynwyd Clowns forevermore." These guys stood by each other in life, and their friendships were a lesson in loyalty I learned at a young age. My family had a slogan too. Ours was "That's my sister." My dad told us to protect and stand up for one another always.

One day in junior high school, I heard that a girl was saying mean things about my sister Cindy. I felt my blood boil and wanted to find this girl to tell her she had to deal with me. I didn't get far since this girl was in high school, a campus I would have to drive to, and I didn't have my license, let alone a car. I never got to give this girl a piece of my mind, but I will always remember the feeling of wanting to protect my sister.

We also had a family handshake. One person would start by squeezing the other person's hand to the beat of "Do you love me?" No words were exchanged. The other person would answer back with a squeeze to the beat of "Yes, I do." The first person would squeeze back to the beat of "How much?" And that's when the receiver would squeeze the person's hand so hard that it almost hurt. The harder the squeeze, the bigger the love. My son Billy put his own spin on the handshake for the next generation by biting my hand, which I take as a complete compliment.

Evidently, I also had a fierce sense of loyalty to Jesus. When I was five years old, my dad's secretary, Susie, came over for dinner one night. Somehow I found out that she was Jewish. When I asked what being Jewish meant, someone in my family (I can't remember who) told me that it was a person who didn't believe in Jesus.

So I locked myself in the bathroom in my house and sang "Jesus Loves Me" over and over again. At five years old this upset me. There was no malice or judgment in the statement that Susie was Jewish. It was said as a fact. But today I feel strongly that it did not need to be said at all.

Thirty nine years later, Susie traveled to Chicago for my daughter Marin's bat mitzvah, and we laughed the entire weekend because this Jesus-singing five-year-old grew up to raise her children Jewish. After all three of my children became a bar and bat mitzvah, my rabbi, Steve Lowenstein, asked me when I was going to become a bat mitzvah. I said, "Anytime! As long as I can keep my man Jesus!"

I guess I am still singing that song but with an unlocked door and an unlocked heart.

When it was time for me to go to college, I attended Lafayette College in Easton, Pennsylvania, because I couldn't escape it. Every time I visited another campus where television was offered as a major, I left saying, "It's not Lafayette." It turns out a total of nine family members attended Lafayette, so anyone in my family who didn't is basically an outsider.

Being an outsider in my family is more like being outstanding because the outsiders went to Duke, Vanderbilt, Northwestern, Columbia, and University of North Carolina Chapel Hill, but we still like them.

My connection to Lafayette and all the joy the school has brought me and my family became more important than the majors that were offered. Lafayette did not have its film and media studies major in 1980. It does now. Lafayette is where my family convenes. Even the outstanding outsiders love Lafayette College. Some families have vacation homes. Our family has Lafayette College.

I was still committed to working in television, so I made Lafayette College work for me. When I was a junior, I took a journalism semester at American University in Washington, DC, and worked for a stringer reporter service on Capitol Hill. I wanted so badly to go to London for that semester, but my dad told me it was too far away and that he would miss me too much, so instead I went to Washington, DC.

That summer I interned at NBC News in Washington, DC, for an evening magazine show called *NBC Monitor* and learned about the Irving B. Harris Internship, a highly coveted paid internship in television production in a city called Chicago. The producer I worked for, Ray Farkas, told me I should apply. I would have never learned about this internship had I gone to London.

Growing up in Philadelphia, I practically never left my back yard, and I went to college an hour from home. I didn't even consider working in any city outside the East Coast. Truthfully, I wasn't even sure I knew where Chicago was. Geography is also not my strong suit. Turns out my husband was on that London semester and we would have met there had I gone. But the universe decided the timing wasn't right.

After my semester and summer in Washington, DC, I returned to Lafayette College for my senior year. While I was gone, an arts center had been built. Show business had finally landed on my campus. Auditions were announced for the first musical to ever be produced titled *Chicago*. I quit the field hockey team and made my way to the audition stage.

I belted out "All that Jazz" in my fishnet stockings with absolutely no training whatsoever, unless you call singing every show tune and Barbra Streisand song ever written at the top of my lungs training … or being on Mr. DB's safety patrol in the fifth grade.

Sadly, I was not cast in *Chicago*, but Chicago was not going away so easily. I applied to the Irving Harris Internship at WTTW-TV in a city called Chicago and got it, proving that Chicago was going to be part of my story one way or another—as long as I could figure out where the hell it was.

That audition moment was all I needed to know that I wanted to be on a stage, maybe not singing or dancing but using my talent in some way. When I was cut from *Chicago*, I decided to take an improv class, one of the bravest things I have ever done. It was that improv class that would pay off for a role I had no idea I would play in Chicago, the city, not the musical.

It turns out my uncle Bill McCarter (member of the Cynwyd Clowns) was the general manager of WTTW-TV in Chicago, the station that offered the internship. I can't make this up, and I literally did not know this fact. What I did know was that my uncle Bill worked in television and that he started his career sweeping the floors at *American Bandstand* at WFIL in Philadelphia.

When he and his family moved to Washington, DC, for a television job, we visited them a few times, but when the McCarters moved to Chicago, we didn't visit them ever because Chicago would have required an airplane. The Oaks family did not travel by air unless it was an emergency. I had no idea the internship I was applying to—and the only one of its kind in the country—was the station where my uncle Bill, who was also my godfather, not only worked but literally ran. The Cynwyd Clowns were at work.

My parents had to make the connection for me. What a complete and total privilege it was, or maybe it wasn't. I was so naïve and thought it would be a good idea to use my godfather's name as a reference. Little did I know at twenty-one that using his name would be the kiss of death for me.

I was told years later by a dear friend who served on the committee that chose the interns that the committee had no intention of hiring me. However, my resume qualified me as one of the top ten candidates, so they agreed to fly me out for an interview. I was also told by a colleague that my godfather walked into the room where the committee was meeting and told them not to give my resume any priority and to treat me just like all the other candidates.

Evidently, I won the committee over, and when I was offered this sought-after internship, I knew I had to work harder than any other intern ever had. And I did.

I am a worker. I always have been. My first sense of knowing I wanted to work was motivated by candy. Betsy, her little brother Ricky, and I would collect all the junk in her house on Saturdays, and go door to door in her neighborhood to try to sell the junk we had collected to her neighbors.

We used whatever money we made to buy candy. We would jump on our banana-seat Schwinn bikes and ride to "the C of G," otherwise known as the center of Gladwyne, and buy as much candy as we could afford at the pharmacy. When I think about Betsy's neighbors now, I feel awful. What did they need with a Barbie without an arm?

When I was eleven years old, I started a day camp with my friend Margie at her house. We recruited all the parents from our church who had children ages three through five years old as clients. We set up our camp every day and ran it like a preschool.

We had circle time, arts and crafts, story time, snack time, and free play, and we even took the kids swimming. This would never happen today. I made more money back then than I knew what to do with, and to date, it's my most favorite job I've ever had.

At sixteen, I worked at a women's clothing boutique called Oodles, and I handled all the inventory. I loved unpacking boxes of cute clothes and hanging them up on rolling racks. Whenever I worked on a makeover show at *The Oprah Winfrey Show*, I always channeled my stock girl from Oodles. Personally, nothing gives me more pleasure than cleaning out and organizing my closet and making it look and smell like Bergdorf Goodman.

One summer I worked at a bank, where one of my real uncles, Uncle Tom, was an executive, which is the only way I was hired. I cried every day. The environment did not please any one of my five senses. It was way too quiet and I count on my fingers. Every branch I worked for seemed to get robbed the week before I arrived, so I was on alert all day and always ready to hide under my desk should robbers storm the bank.

At very young age, I had a burning desire to work in show business. One of my friends, Karen, whom I met in seventh grade and who wore cliffy low-cuts and huckapoo shirts, told me she had the same desire. We used to cry ourselves to sleep at night when we had sleepovers, talking about our fear of never meeting Barbra Streisand or Diana Ross. We were not like the other kids.

We both became television producers, and I had the great honor of meeting both legends at *The Oprah Winfrey Show*. When it was announced that Barbra Streisand was going to be a guest on the show, I called Karen immediately and said, "She's coming." That's all Karen needed to know. She booked her flight and brought her mom with her to Chicago. My mom flew out for the show too.

I remember looking at Karen in the studio and quietly mouthing to her, "We are in the same room as Barbra Streisand!" Our seventh-grade dream had manifested, and not only did we share it with each other, but also we were lucky to share it with our moms too.

Needless to say that I love to work. I just don't love banks or hospitals. I love television studios and theaters. My dad gave me my work ethic because from mighty oaks little acorns grow. It's part of my DNA. It's who I am. I am my father's daughter, a title I wear proudly.

LOVESPEAKS LESSON #6: Be kind, be inclusive, and work hard. Remember that we rise when we lift others. Kindness always builds the mightiest of teams. I have had bosses who were kind and bosses who were not kind. The only way to motivate a team or individuals is through kindness. This is the lesson my dad taught me. And I am so grateful I have grown into the mighty oak I have become.

Be kind to yourself too, especially when you don't get something you want. Remember there is always a reason, and the gift is on its way, even when we can't see the gift right away. I have received a lot of noes recently. Within a few months of receiving the no, I receive the gift. It may not be a big one, but it's always something to be grateful for.

I was not blessed with Broadway skills, but I was blessed with an innate skill of connecting with people, a skill I learned from my father. When I didn't land the role of Velma in *Chicago*, an improv class was sent my way because the universe knew I would need improv training in Chicago for a stage I had no idea was calling my name in a city I didn't yet know, a city where my godfather lived, a city that would invite a woman to host a television show and change the world, a city I would call home for more than thirty-five years, proving you can't stop destiny.

When I didn't get the TEDx Talk I applied for recently, I was devastated, but then I rewrote my stand-up comedy act, and it is way better than any TEDx Talk I could ever give. Don't get me wrong. I still want to stand on a TED stage one day, but I definitely want to stand on a comedy stage too because you can't say fuck on a TED stage. And my stand-up comedy act is fucking hilarious.

SPEAK

What gift did the universe deliver to you that was unexpected?

_____

_____

_____

LOVESPEAKS PRACTICE: Write down what you are grateful for so you can reference everything you have been blessed with. There is nothing more powerful than writing a list. I'm a lover of to-do lists. Writing whatever it is you need to get done or whatever you are grateful for gives you more power to honor your gifts and achieve your dreams. Baby steps are steps. The list doesn't have to get done in a day. It gets done over time, and it is an inspiring way to stay motivated.

Be kind and find a way to unexpectedly bless someone with kindness. Smile at a stranger. Hold the door for someone. Give up your seat on the subway for a person who looks like they could use a seat more than you. Pay for someone's coffee. Let someone into traffic when you see they are having a hard time merging or making a left. Give someone the break they could use because we all could use a break.

I was returning home from a visit with my sister Susan and her grandchildren and waiting in a long Starbucks line at Raleigh Durham International Airport. Behind me were about twenty teens in yellow T-shirts, and I turned around and asked them where they were off to. In that brief moment, every single teenager's face lit up, and in unison they said, "Cuba."

I can't even begin to describe the love I saw on their faces and felt in my heart. So of course, I had to put them on my Instagram story. They told me they were running a vacation Bible study group for children in Cuba, and after I thanked them for spreading love and wished them safe travels, I continued on to find a shorter Starbucks line.

That's when their leader, Michael, came up from behind me and said, "Can I buy your coffee?" I told him he should save his money, and he said, "It makes for a better story! Please let me buy you coffee." Michael was speaking my language, and I was happy to say yes to his unexpected invitation.

Speak to people. Ask people to tell you their stories. Accept kind gestures from people who are leading from their hearts and who are invested in their stories and yours. This is when love speaks.

Is there something you didn't get recently that you really wanted? Write it down. Watch how it comes to you if it's indeed your destiny. Or watch how the right thing comes to you instead of what you thought was right for you. The universe protects us from the things that don't serve us, even when we can't see it ourselves.

ALTERNATIVE LOVESPEAKS PRACTICE: When you don't get something you want, sit with it, and then release it. Let it go. Find a way to celebrate the gift of it being taken away. It wasn't meant for you.

LIVE LOVESPEAKS: Meet Kathleen. My friend Kathleen Sarpy, mother of six and founder and CEO of Agency H5, a communications firm in Chicago, starts her story with "always lead with kindness." Kathleen's success comes straight from her kind heart.

Kathleen is kind to herself, which allows her to be kind to her children, her clients, her Agency H5 staff, her family, her husband, her friends, and strangers. Kathleen believes in inclusion, and she is a shining example of what happens when women support women: kindness flows.

I will never forget standing in the United Center, preparing for *Oprah's Twenty-Fifth Season Surprise Spectacular* when I realized we needed a seat filler for the show that night. We had a million moving parts, and everything was happening in a very short amount of time. When the doors opened, we had to seat fifteen thousand people quickly. We were going to be moving a lot of celebrities and VIPS around in the front row of the audience who would be sitting next to Oprah.

Suddenly, it dawned on me that when Oprah was on the stage, we would need someone to sit in her audience seat next to celebrities like Tom Cruise, Maria Shriver, Gayle King, and Stedman Graham. And that's when I turned to my teammate Dana and said, "Get Kathleen Henson [her name at the time] on the phone. We need her to be our seat filler tonight." Without even considering the fact that Kathleen leads a big company with a long list of clients and more than likely had a full schedule, I acted like this was a normal ask.

Sure enough, Kathleen showed up, looking gorgeous as usual, and she played her part with her professional kindness she has built her career on. She never mentioned what hoops she had to jump through in order to show up on time and camera ready. She just smiled and kindly said, "I'm here!"

In return for her kindness, one of Kathleen's many fun facts is that she can say she was a seat filler for Oprah! No one has supported me in my business more than Kathleen, which is why Kathleen will always be on my team and I will always be Team Kathleen.

You never know who is going to show up for you in your life. Be kind. Welcome what's next. Move on from what didn't happen. We don't have to score every time. We just have to be in the lane that is ours, the lane that starts our story, the lane that is our purpose. Love your lane. Be kind. Keep your door open.

How do you share kindness?

_____

_____

_____

CHAPTER 7

Living Lovespeaks

*Don't be so focused in your plans that you are
unwilling to consider the unexpected.*
—ELIZABETH WARREN

I always knew my dad gave me my heart, but I recently realized he also gave me my unexpected speaker moves. The more unexpected I am when I speak, the more connected I feel to an audience. My *Oprah Winfrey Show* warm-up and my lovespeaks platform are both rooted in the way my dad walked through the halls of his hospital. Connection is always my goal, and it's what defines *living lovespeaks*.

When we connect with ourselves by loving what we do, loving our story, and loving others, we build lives where love speaks. Throw in some unexpected speaker moves, and suddenly our audience is connected, which takes fear out of the equation.

My signature unexpected speaker move is breaking the wall between the speaker and the audience. I like to physically be in the audience as much as possible when I speak. It's unexpected, and it makes me feel comfortable. I think it makes the audience feel comfortable too. It's the coach in me. It's my dad in me. The audience is my team, and I want to be on the field where they are.

Ellen DeGeneres perfected her selfie move to connect with her audience at the Oscars. Michelle Obama allows her audience to finish her sentences. Oprah uses her own story to connect with her audience. Brené Brown connects by being vulnerable. Jimmy Kimmel, my favorite television host, connects with his audience through his heart and humor, and when award shows used to have hosts, he connected through food. Audiences always appreciate a surprise snack.

Audiences also appreciate a giveaway, no matter how big or small. Trust me—I've seen audiences leave a studio with books and leave a studio with cars. No matter what the gift is, the audience leaves with the same feeling, a feeling of surprise and delight.

For the past few seasons, most award shows feature the audience as much as they feature the host and presenters. The Oscars recently went without a host. In my opinion, this shift is because *the better the audience, the better the speaker*, or in this case, the better the audience, the better the award show.

Watch what's happening around you, on television, on social media, online. It's all about the audience, so include your audience when you speak. I promise you will feel a difference, and that difference will make you want to get back on a stage as soon as possible.

Most of us can't just get on a stage for the first time and speak brilliantly like Oprah Winfrey, Brené Brown, or Michelle Obama. We have to practice and gain some momentum before we can feel excitement to speak. What I mean by momentum is this: Start speaking to the people you live with, work with, and spend the most time with. Audience engagement starts at home, so practice your speaking there. And watch your speaking momentum grow.

Speak up in meetings, in church, in temple, in the classroom, or at your dinner table (which can sometimes be a tough audience). Take a public speaking class. Join a community theater group. Do stand-up. Use your voice to step up your speaking game.

I treat every day like *The Oprah Winfrey Show* audience warm-up, whether I am on a stage or not. The world is my audience. It's always show day. Try it for yourself. Practice your timing and wit on the people who surround you in your life. See them. Hear them. Celebrate them. And if you're lucky, make them laugh. Once speaking becomes a daily practice of yours, you will learn to love public speaking.

It doesn't matter if you are a CEO, a celebrity, a super model, a spin instructor, a student, or a stay-at-home mom or dad, speaking well in front of others is not only a career asset, it's a life asset. When we shift the way we think about speaking, we actually begin to look forward to it and have a little fun.

When you speak, share something about yourself, be a little vulnerable and inclusive. Allow your story to give you power and remind yourself how wonderful it is to be a better human. Think about what part of the content in your speech you can relate to and what you feel comfortable sharing with your audience. The minute you share a piece of yourself, you become relatable. Then people feel at ease, and your audience will want to share their energy back with you.

Here's an insider's secret: Your audience wants you to do well. They are rooting for you. This should give every speaker confidence. I once asked an audience in the middle of a speech how I was doing, and the people responded, "Great!" They gave me an unexpected round of applause right in the middle of my speech, and I have to say that it felt really good.

I wasn't planning on asking them the question, but suddenly, I did, and it worked. When you break that wall between you and your audience, you feel good, your audience feels good, and fear feels bad because it can't penetrate the magic you've created.

Nothing says "You will fail" more than silence. Meditation is an exception to the rule. When we are expectedly (or unexpectedly) asked to speak in front of an audience, the expected happens. Terror fills our bodies, and we lose our ability to think because our hearts, the very things we depend on when we speak, are pounding so loud we can't hear our own thoughts.

We have conversations every day with people, and our hearts don't pound, and our palms don't sweat. And yet the minute we are asked to speak and the room goes silent, we lose our minds, and our bodies take over. It's because of silence. Silence is fear's access point. That is why my lovespeaks mantra "The better the audience, the better the speaker" is at the root of fear-free speaking.

When speakers engage their audiences before they speak with a quick mingle and keep the engagement going throughout the speech, the access point for fear is cut off because there is no silence. Hearing other voices in the room not only makes the audience feel comfortable but also makes the speaker comfortable too. Even if you don't engage your audience while you are speaking, mingle with your audience before you speak because if nothing else, mingling is a great speaker warm-up.

A speaker can give it their all on a stage, but if the audience isn't connected, the speech could fall flat. It's like going to a Bruce Springsteen concert and no one dancing. It's just wrong, and it should never happen.

Audiences are expected to engage if the speaker on the stage is expected to perform. Speaking is a two-way street. When one of those streets is blocked, the performance literally bombs on both ends.

Audience members have jobs too. If you are in an audience, remember to pay it forward by being an engaged audience member. I promise you that someone will be an engaged audience member for you too.

When an audience doesn't respond to the talent on the stage, it drives me almost as crazy as when I see audiences seated the wrong way—VIPS in the front rows and fans in the back rows. Who in the world thinks this would make for a better performance?

Connection is the goal when we speak, when we perform, and when we live our lives. Make sure your front rows are filled with fans in everything you do, from speaking to living. But always give love to your back row because you can't have a front row without a back row!

A fellow speaker once told me that a speaker's job is to make the audience want to take you home. If you are expected to speak or perform or you want to live a full life, incorporate any or all my unexpected speaker moves, and watch your audience want to take you home. Literally.

What are you scared of when it comes to speaking? Going blank? Sweating? Losing your place? Sounding stupid? Saying the wrong thing? Being judged? These are all real things to be scared of, and guess what? I've done all of them. My next book could be titled *Stupid Shit Sally Lou Loveman Says*, and yet I still speak with zero fear, proving anyone can do this.

We are all human. Humans sweat. Humans make mistakes. Humans forget. Humans swear. Humans have fear. It's not the mistake our human audience remembers. It's what we as humans do with our mistakes that our audiences never forget. No one is exempt from making mistakes, so use your stumble to your human advantage, and make your mistake brilliant.

I screamed, "Welcome Kenny Loggins," when Kenny Rogers was backstage. I introduced Food Network star Jeff Mauro, known as the Sandwich King, as the Sandwich Queen. I wanted to crawl under the stage both times, but I just smiled and owned it, and the audience immediately embraced me. If you've engaged your audience, they will be there for you, rooting you on, even when you make mistakes.

As they say in show business, "The show must go on!" During one of my preshow warm-up dance parties, a man was doing a *Saturday Night Fever* dance move with his hand and slapped me in the face on the way up by accident. I saw stars, but I didn't stop the warm-up. In fact, I finished it with an ice pack on my face. I am a human. Human faces swell when they are punched. It's okay to ask for an ice pack.

When we took the show to Australia, I told the audience to look under their seats for their fanny packs filled with sunscreen and other items during my audience warm-up. Fanny means vagina to Australians. Aussies call fanny packs bum bags because the word fanny is the front end, not the back end in Oz!

My Instagram friend Anna (@gratitude_sister), who is committed to writing 3,650 days of gratitude in her journal (that's ten years), was in the front row of that audience and says she remembers me from my cute jeans, but I'm pretty sure my fanny pack blunder was more memorable.

I said vagina in front of six thousand people, and they embraced me. Remember that the next time you speak! Anna messaged me recently and said experiencing *The Oprah Winfrey Show* taught her to keep an open mind to wonderful people who could cross her path, which reminds me that humans are ultimately very kind. These same humans make up our audiences. So don't be scared to speak in front of them.

Picture yourself at the end of your speech talking to your audience and seeing and hearing them tell you how well you did. I always picture myself in the destination where I am traveling to along with the people I am visiting or working with whenever I fly. It really helps ease my fear. See the end celebration of your speech, and manifest what is yours.

Bring something that comforts you when you speak, and let it serve as a visual that everything will be okay. I always bring my clipboard when I speak. For you it might be a lucky coin, a meaningful pen, or a piece of jewelry that someone you love gave you. Whatever brings you comfort, bring it along when you speak. Find something that soothes you like meditation or music before you speak, and see if that makes you feel less nervous. It's called distraction. I am a big lover of distraction.

When my favorite airline hired me to speak on a plane, I said, "Wait. You want me to do something I fear while I'm doing something I love ... and pay me?" I couldn't say yes fast enough. I was allowed to use the flight attendant intercom and became so distracted with speaking to the passengers and completely caught up in my purpose that I didn't realize we were taking off.

The crew had to tell me to sit down and buckle up! I was doing something I loved, speaking, which helped me avoid thinking about something I loathe, flying.

Look for distractions to help dodge your fear and keep you from the fetal position. Look for your purpose. If I am speaking on a plane or writing on a plane, I am in my purpose, and I have no fear. On a flight back from New York, I was seated next to a ten-year-old boy who was traveling as an unaccompanied minor. My team felt bad for me, and I told them, "Are you kidding me! This is my dream seatmate!"

The weather was so bad and this child was so scared that he ended up throwing up in my lap. I didn't care. I was in mom purpose, and I was taking care of him. I suggested we play hangman. My puzzle was "High School Musical." His was "Get Me off This Plane." Whatever your purpose is, use it when you speak because fear can never penetrate purpose and positive distraction is always the best way to circumvent fear.

If you are scheduled to speak, fill your day with things that make you happy and warm you up. Schedule a meeting you know will go well. Have a conversation with a friend who builds you up and makes you laugh and reminds you that life goes on no matter how your speech goes. It's just a speech. No one ever died from a bad speech.

Go for a run. Blast Beyoncé. Do whatever it is that makes you feel good. Just make some noise. A busy brain has no time for fear. Downtime and silence is what allows fear to creep in. And when you take the stage, imagine fire coming out of your heels like you just got there because *you've got this.* No big deal.

If you are traveling to speak, find out as much as you can about the city where you are speaking. Talk to your Uber driver, the hotel staff, your blow-dry bar stylist, or people in the neighborhood. Look for signs in storefronts, and google what the city is best known for. Incorporate what you learn into your speech, and show your audience that you care not only about them but also about their community.

Once you have the confidence of knowing you are supposed to be on that stage, add in some unexpected moves. As speakers, we need to be engaged and prepared, but we must always leave room for the unexpected. Schedule time in your speech for this extra engagement.

We already know a podium feels safe because it is a place where we can hide. We can hide our script, and we can hide ourselves. Consider stepping away from the podium, and surprise your audience by eliminating that barrier.

When you break that wall with your audience, your audience immediately leans in, and they are more engaged. You don't have to leave the podium for your entire speech, but if the stage allows for you to freely walk away from that safe zone, try it.

If you need your script for comfort, make a note in your script in a place where it would be a good time for you to walk away and be comfortable speaking without it. You can always go back to your home base.

As speakers we think we have to do all the speaking. But in order to be a good speaker, we have to be good listeners. Listen to your audience. Listen to what they share with you before you speak and what they may even share with you while you are speaking.

My favorite speaker tip is to let the room determine the order of your speech, not your script. Don't be so locked to your script that you can't alter it a bit when something unexpected happens.

If someone speaks before you and covers content you have included in your speech, eliminate it, and keep it moving. If someone from your audience asks a question about content you plan to cover later, cover it in the moment, and eliminate it later. In other words, be willing to wing it sometimes because that's what makes a speaker memorable.

Welcome interruptions. They are unexpected gold. When I presented at Chicago Ideas, my rabbi walked into the room. It was a total surprise to me that he was attending my talk, and as I was just about to begin, I saw him enter the back of the room. I immediately said, "I can't fail today because God just walked in. Everyone, please welcome my rabbi, Steven Lowenstein!"

Everyone laughed. I felt completely confident, and the audience felt completely comfortable. The only joke a speaker should ever tell is a joke that could only happen live. You can't plan for a joke, but when the opportunity is there for you to take, take it. Just keep it clean. Trust me—I struggle with clean, which is why I love stand-up.

Remember to thank your audience. A simple thank-you for showing up really makes an impact on an audience. I start every speech by saying thank you, and I always ask the audience to thank one another for showing up. It allows for some audience connection and also for a moment of gratitude. Showing up is a big deal, and it should be recognized. If we don't show up, the room is empty, and that's never good for a speaker.

SPEAK

Since we already know that compliments inspire us all to perform at our best, compliment your audience. You want your audience to perform well so you can too, so compliment them. When my Shred415 instructors Jordyn and Kim say, "You've got this, Sally Lou," I run faster on the treadmill. When my Spynergy Winnetka instructor Jen tells our class we are in great shape, we believe her, and we turn our dials on the bikes to the right and work harder.

You want your audience to work harder for you, so disarm them with kindness, use their names, and give them compliments. You can feel the energy in the room change with a compliment just like you can feel it change on a plane.

For those of you who are SoulCycle fans like I am, think of yourself as a SoulCycle instructor when you speak. A SoulCycle class reminds me of my *Oprah Winfrey Show* warm-up, including the sweat.

Meet Joshua. My favorite SoulCycle instructor. Joshua begins class by saying, "How we doing today?" I love the use of the word *we*. It's so inclusive. When he asks his riders a question, he offers us two answers—yes and yes. He connects the room by calling our class a *team*, and he makes a huge effort to create a community by reminding us we are all in this together and surrounded by new friends.

He shares a little bit about himself, which makes us all want to know more, and his signature "Add love" means that we should add to our dial and work harder. And we do it because we've all signed up for love. He is like a conductor waving his arms from his bike, and we are his instruments riding to his rhythm. Well, at least everyone else except me.

Joshua engages his audience (a.k.a. his riders) the same way I engage any audience, which is why I always say I would be the best SoulCycle instructor if I could just get the cycling and choreography down.

The candle tradition at the end of class is what I love the most. At the beginning of every speech or audience warm-up I perform, I always pick an audience captain. Someone who has beautiful energy or someone who looks like they could use a lift, which reminds me of the candle offering.

Choose someone in your audience to be your captain, announce it to the room, and watch how the support from one person travels throughout the audience. Inclusion and connection is what makes magic real.

Basically, if you want to be a good speaker, take a SoulCycle class when you finish this book, and study the teacher. Use his or her unexpected moves of connection in your next speech, and some of mine, and watch your audience want to take you home.

LOVESPEAKS LESSON #7: The better the audience, the better the speaker. If you want your audience to be engaged, connect with them before you speak, and throw in some unexpected speaker moves. Let love speaks through your engagement with the audience. Use content you've collected from the audience prior to your talk as an unexpected way of connecting with them from the stage. And always remember to be a good audience member when you're not on the stage.

What is your unexpected speaker move?

_____

_____

_____

LOVESPEAKS PRACTICE: Participate in the world, and use your heart daily. Try an unexpected move in your life before you try it out on a stage. Compliment someone, ask the cashier at a store how their day is going when they are ringing up your purchases, speak to people who look like they could use a smile and practice eye contact with people. Unhinge people from their normal lives, and grace them with some unexpected love.

Record the unexpected moves you make and choose the one that feels most comfortable to you. Practice your move, and maybe you will find yourself using it on a stage when you speak.

ALTERNATIVE LOVESPEAKS PRACTICE: We live in a world where we are more connected than ever, but we are also very protective of our space. It's not always comfortable for people to insert themselves into another person's life. This is how I live, so I don't see it as anything but normal, and I understand that I am not normal.

If you are not comfortable with speaking to a stranger, try the suggested practices with people you already know. And take a

SoulCycle class! Fill your soul, burn some calories, be a part of a community, and leave a better speaker and a better human.

LIVE LOVESPEAKS: I will never forget watching the commencement speaker at my daughter Carly's high school graduation leave the podium and deliver his speech to a crowd of 1,200 students and an audience of eight thousand. I was standing on my feet and cheering for him because he was using an unexpected speaker move at a young age and it was so brave.

Meet Jordan. The speaker's name is Jordan, and it won't shock you that I inserted myself into his life as soon as the ceremony ended. I wanted to know everything about his process and how he decided to leave the podium and deliver his speech in the audience. He told me he was inspired by Brené Brown's TED talk about vulnerability and stepping into the arena. So he decided to step into the arena himself, literally. Today Jordan is one of my speaker heroes because he was so brave at eighteen and continues to be brave in his speaking career.

Brave moves move us forward. Be brave. Take the power and momentum you feel when you are being brave (no matter what that brave thing is), and let it serve you when you are speaking.

Every time I speak, I think about the photo I took on top of the Sydney Harbor Bridge in Australia. I was terrified being on the top of a bridge suspended over open water, boats, and traffic. But I climbed that bridge for one reason—to be brave, to be a better speaker, and to be able to tell the story. The first trip I took to Sydney I said no the the invitation to climb the bridge. The second trip I said yes. Be brave. Accept invitations from people who love or like you. Be a better speaker and a happier human.

Look for brave things to do that push you out of your comfort zone so you can use that power to be more comfortable on a stage and in life. And before you take the stage, repeat these two very important mantras to yourself: "I've got this," and "I am supposed to be here." You will begin to believe both.

What is your bravest moment?

_____

_____

_____

CHAPTER 8

Stories from the Red Seat

When the whole world is silent, even one voice becomes powerful.
—MALALA YOUSAFZAI

I guess I was supposed to be in Chicago in 1984. Had my dad allowed me to go to the semester abroad in London, I would have never gone to Washington, DC, which means I would have never learned about the Irving Harris Internship and I would have never moved to Chicago. The universe took care of putting me in the same city at the same time as a woman named Oprah Winfrey.

My *Mike Douglas Show* experience was the invitation I was given to open the door to a career in television, and now my first television job placed me in the same city as a woman who would change not only the face of television but also the world. I would call this a God moment.

This was my chance to be part of something really big, to be in my purpose, and to impact people's lives. This was my own "Dr. Oaks" moment. This was my show day, even though I had no idea how big this opportunity was at the time.

I first met Oprah when she was a guest on our local news show at WTTW, *Chicago Tonight.* I was the production assistant in charge of taking her to her green room. I remember she complimented my white blouse as I escorted her down the hallway. Two years later, when Oprah launched *The Oprah Winfrey Show*, I interviewed with her for the audience coordinator position. My friend Marcy's sister's friend Charlotte worked for ABC and gave my resume to the executive producer, and I was called in for an interview with Oprah and the executive producer.

I liked Oprah immediately, of course. She complimented my navy suit. It was not your typical interview suit. It was a belted tunic over a skirt with massive shoulder pads. It was 1986, and yes, I still have it. The '80s were the best decade, and I always tell my kids how sorry I am that they never got to experience them. When something isn't as good as it used to be, I always say, "The '80s are over."

My interview went well, but I didn't get the job. I was kind of shocked. One year later the executive producer called me and offered me the same job, audience coordinator, proving a closed door is never closed forever if it is meant to be your destiny, and I accepted the invitation to join a journey of a lifetime.

The crew at WTTW said the reason I left was because I didn't want to repeat an outfit at work. While I appreciate a good joke and am completely comfortable being made fun of, I really had no idea the transformation my life was about to take, but I knew it would be greater than a cute outfit, and for me, that's saying a lot!

During my years at Harpo, I always knew I was called to work for Oprah. It was a privilege to have been able to call her my boss and impact people's lives through her show and her network. In the same way my former boss complimented my blouse and my interview suit, she complimented my work over the years, which meant everything to me. It still does.

From the first day I met Oprah, I felt her grace and her magic. It's impossible to miss. That magic played a big role in the *Oprah* studio. It wasn't the kind where rabbits get pulled out of hats but the kind you can't explain.

I was promoted to show producer in 1989. I didn't want the job, but who says no to that kind of opportunity? I knew I was better suited for the studio and working with audiences. My dream started in a studio audience seat, and I didn't want to leave that seat, but I said yes.

As soon as I became a producer, I knew I was in over my head. I spent a lot of time crying in the bathroom. The idea of a guest canceling gave me so much anxiety. Having to tell my executive producer I had nothing booked for the live show made me feel a sense of doom that made me stop loving my job.

I ended up quitting my job as a producer because I didn't want to fail. When I wasn't hired to return as a freelancer at Harpo, which I thought was the plan, I took another job at another new talk show as a producer, even though I didn't want to be a producer. My time there wouldn't last long because the host was about as real as the cardboard cutout I walked by every morning to get to my new office. You can't work for Oprah and then work for someone else who isn't the real deal. So I quit that job too.

Luckily for me, I was invited back to freelance for *The Oprah Winfrey Show* a year later and happily worked part-time as an associate producer for the next ten years while I had babies. I was able to be home with my kids when I wasn't assigned to work on a show and kept my face on the producers' radar, which allowed me the opportunity to return to full-time work when the right opportunity was available.

All my children made appearances on *The Oprah Winfrey Show*, one of their fun facts. My fun fact is that I am an Emmy Award-winning producer. I was a producer for one year, a year we won an Emmy, making me the most undeserving winner of an Emmy ever. I won by association.

My Emmy sits on my shelf at home, and when I look at it, I think about my times on *The Oprah Winfrey Show* stage warming up the audience or seating the audience or managing huge audiences on our remote shows or stopping a fight or holding onto people as they waited for the ambulance or giving love to people in big ways and small, and the I'm okay with having it. But I would never call myself an Emmy Award-winning producer—unless Emmy Awards were given to audience producers.

After ten years of freelancing at Harpo, three producer friends and mentors, Lisa, Ellen, and Dianne, asked me to come back full-time as the audience producer. I threw myself into that role like a producer would, and I loved every minute in that seat because it was my seat. Sometimes we have to sit in the wrong seat to understand where our right seat is. The red seat was my seat.

I may have not been saving lives like my father, but I was helping to celebrate them and making them better every day I was on *The Oprah Winfrey Show* stage. And I could certainly do that as the person with the tickets—the one thing everyone wanted that money couldn't buy.

I used to worry how we would ever fill the seats when we were *live* every day in Chicago, a city with snowstorms. We used to pull out the black duvetyn drape to cover the empty seats when we couldn't fill the audience. That would quickly change.

My new worry was how would we ever get everyone in who wanted to see the show. It would keep me up at night. When I meet people today who tell me they never saw *The Oprah Winfrey Show* in the studio, it literally crushes me.

There was nothing I loved more than giving tickets to people, especially unexpectedly. Whenever I traveled, I looked for people who were kind or doing their jobs really well or just needed an extra lift in their day. I felt like Santa Claus.

One time I was on a plane going to Philadelphia, and a woman was sitting next to me and crying the entire flight. I asked her if she was okay, and she explained that she was going to see her young son whom she had lost custody to and who was now living in Philadelphia with his father. I didn't ask her the details. I just listened to her story.

When we landed in Philadelphia, I gave her my business card and told her that she was going to need something to look forward to when she got on the plane to come back to Chicago. I had not mentioned that I worked for *The Oprah Winfrey Show,* but when she saw my card, I said, "Bring a friend to the show." Her tears stopped, and I saw a small smile emerge onto her face. I wasn't saving her life. I was just making her life a little better.

We all need a reason to get back on the plane sometimes, and having something to look forward to always helps. I miss the power of that gift every day. But we all have the power to add our own value to people's lives—a smile, a compliment, a hug, a joke, or just helping someone who is carrying too many bags get up a flight of stairs. Let's do more of that.

That love of connection comes straight from the people who poured love into my heart, the people I write about in this book, the people who built the stage for my love to speak.

*T*he Oprah Winfrey Show gave me the team my father had prepared me for, a team that through thick and through thin, worked hard and played hard. We were a work family that shared one motto, "Teamwork makes the dream work." There was nothing we couldn't do as long as we were doing it together. We were a team of love laborers, and I am so grateful to have been a small part of so much history.

In season twenty-five, we taped two *Favorite Things* shows back to back. As the first audience was leaving, the second audience saw them leaving with *Favorite Things* bags. What the second audience didn't know was that they were getting *Favorite Things* too! One *Favorite Things* show was a lot to manage for our production team, but two was insane. That's how we rolled in season twenty-five.

The weekend before the tapings, I hosted our annual audience team holiday party at my house. I turned my garage into a disco and called it Club Down Under because we were heading to Australia in a few weeks to tape two shows with our ultimate viewers, and so I surprised my team with an unexpected dance party.

The second surprise came when we all woke up with food poisoning the next morning. We were dropping like flies. I have no idea how it happened, but it happened. During our back-to-back *Favorite Things* tapings, my team and I were throwing up in the bathroom and coming back into the studio to work the shows because teamwork makes the dream work. I basically poisoned my team, and they still showed up to work and gave it their all.

When we were preparing for *Oprah's Twenty-Fifth Season Surprise Spectacular*, we were booking audiences for huge shows in the studio as well as ticketing the fifteen-thousand-person stadium audience. The process of ticketing our own studio audience was a job in and of itself, but taking on fifteen thousand seats in a venue that wasn't our home was an enormous task, so I hired a few freelancers to help.

When the freelancers arrived in my office, I asked them if they could read my mind because I didn't have time to explain what needed to get done. And basically, they did. They got to work, and my talented team along with those talented freelancers ticketed fifteen thousand people in under ten days. All you had to do was step into the building, and suddenly, magic was bestowed upon you. The building was a magnet for talent, and that talent created magic.

The day before the show, my parents were in town because my entire family flew in to attend *Oprah's Surprise Spectacular*. They came over to our office, and my dad gave my team a "Dr. Oaks" preshow pep talk. I've heard my dad give pep talks to every sports team I have ever played on, but this talk was different because this was *my* team. I could see my team's faces looking at him and thinking, *Now we understand Sally Lou.*

On the day of the show, we arrived at the United Center, and I remember one of my teammates pulling me by the shoulders and saying, "Sally Lou, this wall is blocking two hundred seats." It didn't even register to me that a wall had been built without us knowing and the two hundred seats that had already been ticketed were now blocked. But my team spoke "Sally Lou," which made us very efficient.

This is why we need a team—to shake us until we understand that something needs to be resolved immediately. I don't remember how we did it. I just know it had something to do with putting a halt on distributing our standby tickets and repurposing those tickets to the people whose views were now blocked. I think I blacked out, but I know my team handled the solution beautifully.

Your team does not have to act like you or think like you, and they don't have to have the same talents you have. In fact, the less you are alike, the more likely you are to be invincible.

While I always supported my team, I wasn't always easy on them. I expected a lot. For example, there was the time we were in Australia and we were preparing twelve thousand tickets for distribution to two audiences at the forecourt of the Sydney Opera House. Nicole and Dana were working together to prepare the tickets. Nicole was eating an apple, and I said, "Nicole, either eat the apple or rip the tickets." It wasn't the nicest way to handle it, but we managed to laugh about it later. I allowed my stress to speak, which is never good. But as long as we are laughing, we are moving forward.

One thing my team would all say is that I wanted them to develop their unique talents and use those talents to benefit not only the team but also themselves. They have all successfully done so, and each person has a "do what you love" and lovespeaks story to tell. That makes me happy and I am so proud of my team.

There is nothing more powerful than show day. Everything is elevated, and there is an electricity in the air you can physically feel. Imagine the Black Eyed Peas' "I've Got a Feeling" playing in your head on a loop. That's the kind of electricity I'm talking about. It's a day when you are filled with excitement, purpose, and skill, ready to perform at your absolute best and maybe even transform lives.

You don't have to be in the *Oprah* studio to feel the power of show day. I treat every day like it's show day, and you can too. Life gives us so many reasons to celebrate this feeling—playing on a sports team, landing a client you've been working so hard to get, giving birth to your child, breaking a habit that was wasn't serving you, serving others, writing a book, reading a book, running a marathon, finishing your master's degree. You fill in the blank for whatever your show day is.

For me, walking up the marble staircase at Harpo Studios every morning and hearing the quiet of the building at six thirty was never lost on me. I felt the importance of being in the building. I almost felt selfish when I left my house at five forty-five in the morning to go to work. I was living my dream, my purpose, my show day, and my husband was making beds, packing lunches, walking the dog, taking our kids to school, and going to work.

The smell of Oprah's flatiron and hairspray meant it was show day, a day we would be transforming lives, a day of purpose. Interestingly, research says that smell is closely linked to our memory and that women have a better sense of smell than men do. I clearly have a high-functioning sense of smell, and I have relied on this gift to direct me to my purpose.

The quiet of the building wouldn't last long. Soon it would move from quiet to show day. The building would be filled with the buzz of producers, challenges, surprises, excitement, laughter, tears, giveaways, gratitude, and applause, lots and lots of applause.

Sometimes there were so many exciting things happening at once in the building that it was hard to take it all in. Tom Cruise jumped on the couch. An entire studio audience was given cars. People's homes were paid off. Celebrities surprised their fans. Oprah shared her wisdom, and regular people like you and me told their stories and changed the world.

One night my team and I were working late in my office and living our best lives. We were finishing up the final seating for *Oprah's Surprise Fiftieth Birthday* show when my office phone rang. It was Lisa, a producer and mentor, asking me to come down to the studio quickly because there had been some big changes.

I grabbed my clipboard and went running to the studio. I am pretty clumsy. (If you've worked with me you, know this). I was moving fast too. I got to the studio, and suddenly, I slammed into a body. It was me, my clipboard, and a body. I looked up, and that body was—you got it—John Travolta!

There I was in the most celebrated television talk show studio of all time with my clipboard and my pretend boyfriend who had canceled on me in 1976. All I could think about was my mom and how grateful I was that she took the time to invite me to a television show that would change my life forever and that I had taken the time to say yes.

I also thought about the girl with the clipboard, and maybe she would be proud too. Tears were pouring down my face, and I can only imagine that John Travolta thought I was crazy.

This was my professional full-circle moment. I could have said, "Good night, everyone," and retired from television, but that wouldn't be a forward move. This was momentum, and it served me in ways I could have never imagined. It was also a really good end to one of my favorite stories.

Before my John Travolta reunion, I had another moment that stays on my heart. It was 1989, and we took the show to Charleston, South Carolina, to cover Hurricane Hugo. We were a small team of producers back then, and we all went out to dinner. When we returned to the hotel, we got onto the elevator to go back to our rooms. We were exhausted, and people were saying good night as they got off on their respective floors. We had an early call for the show in the morning, and we needed sleep.

I noticed there was a man on the elevator with us. He may have been a lovely man, but we didn't know him and I knew that Oprah was continuing on past my floor. I vividly remember thinking to myself that there was no way I was getting off that elevator on my floor and leaving her alone with this man. In that moment I knew I was taking the ride with her. This was 1989, a very different time, but a feeling I will never forget because "That's my sister" extends to all people I love.

And that ride sure was a good one. Working for Oprah was like getting a master's degree in living your best life, doing what you love, spirituality, and wellness. I was taught kindness, forgiveness, gratitude, and hard work. My career opened my world up to experiences I could have never dreamed of at age fourteen.

I have been able to hit career highs in the field of my dreams with the best team in television. I have been able to directly impact people's lives through the show and now through my own lovespeaks platform. I have had the privilege of hearing Oprah's words and wisdom firsthand and have successfully incorporated them into my life. I have traveled the country and the world. And I was lucky to have been able to include my children, husband, family, and friends in the excitement of my career.

My children's lives have been made better by the very fact that Oprah Winfrey was my boss. I will never forget the feeling I had when I came home and told my kids and husband that Oprah was taking the staff and their families to Hawaii for a week. Here I was, a working mom who felt a lot of guilt about the time I spent away from my family, and I was able to come home and say that because of my career and my incredible boss, I was able to give my family an invitation of a lifetime.

Yes, the week in Hawaii was outstanding, but the power I felt giving the invitation to my family is the gift I will never forget.

When Oprah launched her network OWN, The Oprah Winfrey Network, we traveled to Houston to tape *Oprah's Lifeclass*. During our audience load, an usher at the venue asked if she could speak with me. Her name was Carmen. I said, "Yes, of course," and then Carmen said, "I have a book." Well, I am pretty sure it was my turn to roll my eyes because everyone has a book for Oprah.

I was already trying to figure out how I was going to politely say that I couldn't accept her book. And that's when she stopped me and said, "No, I didn't write a book. Let me show you." She reached into her backpack and handed me a coffee table book that was wrapped in bubble for protection. I could see the book was old from the yellowing cover. The title of the book was *I Dream a World: Portraits of Black Women Who Changed America*.

Carmen told me she had purchased the book twenty-three years prior, and it was her mission to get as many signatures as possible from the women featured in the book. When she turned to Rosa Parks's page and showed me Rosa Parks's signature, I knew I had to make Carmen's dream come true.

So I immediately got in touch with Oprah's executive team and brought them the book. Next thing you know, Carmen was brought backstage where she met Oprah. Oprah also signed her book with a beautiful message, and they talked for a few minutes.

When I found Carmen after her big moment, she shook in my arms and thanked me. She told me that this book would be the greatest treasure she would pass down to her children and grandchildren.

I wasn't saving lives. I was just making them better. Connecting Carmen to her dream was my own little show day within show day.

Around every corner at Harpo Studios, there was usually a celebrity sighting or a moment that stirred your soul, which added to the magic. In 1990, we had recently moved into the building, and I remember it felt so big. I thought we would never fill the space. Years later we would become a campus with many buildings, including a retail store, a café, a spa, and a gym. Tom Cruise came to the show to promote his film *Days of Thunder*. He had just announced he was dating Nicole Kidman, but for twenty minutes Tom Cruise was mine.

I was assigned to his green room, and he asked me for a tour of our new studio. Naturally, I obliged. We walked the space, just the two of us. No entourage. No security. Just me and Tom Cruise. Trust me—I took my time. He touched the small of my back two times as we passed through doorways. Tom Cruise's charm was intoxicating, and in that moment I just drank in his Hollywood charm.

One morning I was taping reserved cards on the seats in the studio during Kelly Clarkson's sound check. She was singing "Because of You." I was the only person in the studio besides the crew. When I realized what was happening, I sat down in the front row in one of those magical red seats, and Kelly Clarkson serenaded me. I literally sobbed.

When Michael Bublé was doing his sound check for "Haven't Met You Yet," I was so engrossed in reading the script to prepare for my warm-up, I didn't realize Michael Bublé was singing to me until I looked up and saw his adorable face. More tears.

I was in the studio when Beyoncé Knowles, Kelly Rowlands, and Michelle Williams were rehearsing their reunion performance of their Destiny's Child hit "Lose My Breath" on treadmills. There. Are. No. Words.

One afternoon my team and I were having a meeting in my office. My desk faced the outside hallway, and in the middle of our meeting, I saw Oprah Winfrey and Bill Gates walk by. I stopped the meeting so we could take the moment in.

In 1999 I was asked to be on a mom panel for a series called *Great Mom Getaways*. We featured moms who were doing great things and celebrated them by sending them off on much-needed vacations. It was April, and I had just given birth to my son Billy the month before.

My friend and show hairstylist Vivian watched Billy in the green room while I was a guest on the show. When the show ended, I came racing back into the green room to breastfeed Billy. I went into the small makeup room that was off the green room, and when I came out of the makeup room with Billy, I discovered a prayer circle in progress. Gary Zukav, author of *The Seat of the Soul*, was a guest on the next show, and he was holding a prayer circle in the green room. He invited me and Billy to join them.

It was April of 1999, and the Columbine shooting had just happened. I entered the quiet circle and joined hands with the person who was standing next to me. The person on the other side of me took Billy's one-month-old hand in hers. It was powerful. All I could think about were the children, the mothers of the children, the fathers of the children, the siblings of the children, and the grandparents of the children. I have not stopped praying since that moment.

This is what life was like working at Harpo Studios. It was completely and totally magical. Seeing celebrities was always fun, but seeing people's lives transform when they shared their stories on the show was life-changing. We had to literally stop and take in all that was happening because it was bigger and brighter than anyone could ever try to explain. The building changed people. It changed the world. It changed me.

Even though the building is now the corporate office headquarters for McDonald's, the magic that happened inside that building lives in me and in every person who ever had the privilege of working there.

When I found out that the building was being torn down, I started to have dreams about it. I remember the Easter Sunday before the building actually came down, waking up and crying from a dream I had about the building. How could all that history be taken away?

A few weeks later, I drove over to the building when the wrecking ball was at work. I parked my car and walked into the parking lot where employees had parked their cars and where we hid the 276 Pontiac G6s, the ones with the giant red bows. Tears were running down my face. I asked a construction worker if I could take a brick. Then I took another one ... and another one.

I took as many bricks as I could carry, and I gave them to some of my audience teammates—a team I had built brick by brick and had loved and cried and laughed with, a team I had worked so hard with. "You get a brick. You get a brick! Everybody gets a brick!"

I wish for all of us to love a career so much and see it so clearly that we would be willing to carry a brick for our team. Yes, the building came down, but the magic didn't. That magic lives in all of us for life.

I used to annoy my team so much when we took the show on the road. We would be in the middle of packing up our supplies, and I would say, "Did we pack the wristbands, gaffer's tape, Sharpies, blue cards, and paper? Did we pack the Oprah magic?"

And my team would roll their eyes at me and say, "Yes, Sally Lou, we packed the Oprah magic."

But that magic was real. We carried that magic to every show we produced, and we carry that magic to our next careers, to our next opportunities, to our children, and to our families. That's where the magic lives, and I will always be grateful that I was invited to be one of Oprah's magic makers.

I am proud to say I am one of a small group of people who had the privilege of working for every single executive producer of *The Oprah Winfrey Show*—Debbie, Dianne, Ellen, Lisa, and Sheri. Each one left a magical mark on me forever.

Some people call it coincidence or luck. I call it magic. How else can you explain twenty-three thousand people learning a flash mob dance in under an hour, 276 Pontiac G6s given away to one audience without anyone knowing, a minivan with four ultimate viewers arriving with precision timing onto *The Oprah Winfrey Show* set, reuniting a Rwandan family, two hundred men who were sexually abused as young boys standing together in unity, or getting America to read?

Yes, we worked our asses off. Yes, the talent pool was extraordinary. Yes, the viewers were loyal with their love. And yes, Oprah is a gifted human I truly believe was sent straight from God. This perfect combination of everything being in alignment made the magic real. The voices that spoke up on the show, starting with the host, and the audience who spoke from the red seats changed the world because our stories have power, even when it's just one voice. Use yours.

LOVESPEAKS LESSON #8: Look for magic in your life. Find magic in your work, your children, your grandchildren and through service. Imagine yourself sitting in one of Oprah's red seats, and welcome magic into your life. Make time for stillness so you can let more magic in.

When things fall into place and you can't explain it, that's a sign of magic. When you put good energy into the universe daily, you open the door to magic. Welcome magic into your life, and watch how your life unexpectedly changes for the better.

Where do you find your magic?

_____

_____

_____

LOVESPEAKS PRACTICE: Recognize magic in the ordinary. Write down the magical things that happen to you. Magic can't be explained, so don't try to explain it. Just welcome it into your life and notice it so you can open yourself up to more.

ALTERNATIVE LOVESPEAKS PRACTICE: If you don't believe in magic, look for it, and see if you can be convinced otherwise. I know it's there. I've seen it too many times.

LIVE LOVESPEAKS: When a talented group of people comes together for one purpose and are led by a leader who embodies that purpose, magic happens. You can't plan for it or even train for it. It can only happen when everything is in alignment.

Magic is not reserved for *The Oprah Winfrey Show*. Magic is reserved for anyone who is willing to see it and embody it. Magic happens in corporations, nonprofits, church and temple congregations, and families. I see it at my temple, AM Shalom (led by Rabbi Steven Lowenstein), at my church, Christ Church (led by Rector Christopher Powell), in my family of origin (led by my father and mother), in my own family (led by my husband and me), and at a nonprofit where I volunteer my time, Erika's Lighthouse, that helps teens talk about depression (led by founders Ginny and Tom Neuckranz).

These are the magic makers in my life. Look for the magic makers in yours.

How are you putting your energy out into the world to make magic?

_____

_____

_____

CHAPTER 9

Love Your Audience

*Courage is what it takes to stand up and speak; courage
is also what it takes to sit down and listen.*
—WINSTON CHURCHILL

The *Oprah Winfrey Show* audience was everything to me. The
people who attended the show didn't just fill the seats. They
filled my soul. The audience became family and friends with one
another, with me, and with my team. We took the time to listen
to their stories. We got to know them as people, not just fans. And because
of all the listening and sharing we did, friendships were formed. So many
fabulous former audience members have gone above and beyond attending
the show and have impacted my life and made me a better human.

- John Richards was kind enough to write an admissions letter for
  my daughter Marin when she applied to Vanderbilt University, and
  she was accepted.
- Cheryl Jackson hired me to emcee her Minnie's Food Pantry
  Gala, where I fell in love with her friends and family as well as her
  purpose to provide meals for families in need with dignity.
- Will Hudson wowed me so much from his red audience seat at the
  show and continues to wow me with inspirational messages.
- I plucked Mara Davis out of the Caesar's Palace lobby in Las Vegas
  and gave her tickets to the show as a surprise and sat her in the
  front row. She was a complete stranger to me at the time, and
  today she is one of my biggest lovespeaks supporters. I dream of
  hosting a podcast with her because she is hilarious. I call it *Davis
  Love, Not the Golfer.*

- Liz Toole referred the Advancing Women in Trucking speaking opportunity to me, which was my first international gig.
- Sam Raoof and Justine Movson invited me to their wedding.
- Jodi Beals invited me to speak at Groupon.
- Tierra Destiny Reid invited me to facilitate a lesson on how speaking our stories heal us for her When Women Heal platform.
- Megan Castran invited me to visit her in Melbourne, Australia, and she fills every day with rainbows and happy faces.
- Nada Smith booked me as a guest for an XM Radio show with the fabulous host Shaun Proulx.
- Brittney Cammack passed along the resume of my talented friend with his fashion degree to her famous fashion designer cousin.
- Paolo Presta went from the famous red seat in *The Oprah Winfrey Show* audience to an outstanding host of *Spoonful of Paolo*, and he fills me with joy every time he posts on Facebook or Instagram because his love speaks so loudly.
- Prasanna Ranganathan's love glowed so bright when he attended the show, and it continues to brighten the world. When I picture Prasanna, I literally see the color yellow.
- Erin Abbot and Brian Wefel traveled to Chicago to attend my Unexpected Speaker workshop.
- Ursula Jones was bold enough to ask me to put her in the front row of the audience, and she leads her life in that beautiful, brave, and bold way as a successful attorney.
- Jasmine Stringer, Charity Washington, Marisa Tigney, Lonnell Williams, Jill Cruse, Kimberly Clay, and Janet Auty-Carlisle all live their lives with love and remind me to let my love speak.

I am positive I have left many people I adore off this list, and I apologize. These are just a handful of names of the many people who have touched and continue to touch my heart.

I have boxes of thank-you notes from audience members I cherish. Thank-you notes are a lost art, and I suggest to all millennials reading—and midlifers too—to write handwritten thank-you notes and grab someone's attention. It is always the right thing to do.

I also have a shoebox of the thank-you notes from Oprah. After every show, she wrote the producer a thank-you note. Name one other person in television who has ever done that. You can't. There's only one.

Social media was in its infancy during the final years of *The Oprah Winfrey Show*, and I am so grateful it wasn't like it is today. Social media, in my opinion, would have taken away some of the magic. But I am also grateful social media is like it is today because Facebook and Instagram help keep these connections close.

So many of the hundreds and thousands of people who came through that studio were living their best lives and continue to live them well today. When you attended *The Oprah Winfrey Show*, you were already invested in living your best life.

People told us that they had scheduled pedicures in preparation for the show, even though Oprah would never see their feet. That was *The Oprah Winfrey Show* audience. They brought it all when they arrived, from head to toe and inside and out. Not only did it show up on the air, but it showed up in real life too.

My intention for the preshow warm-up was to make the connection with the audience deeper. I could have stood on the stage and told people where the exits were, and the audience would have still gone crazy when Oprah entered the studio. But I wanted something more. I wanted people to really feel like they were seen and heard—a lesson I learned from my boss and my father.

I wanted the audience to experience what it felt like to be with the person they loved the most, the person they called first when they got their *Oprah Winfrey Show* tickets, inside Oprah's studio. Every Oprah fan has a person they called to say, "Are you watching *Oprah*?" That was what I wanted to create for the warm-up. That was the experience I wanted everyone to walk away with and hold onto forever just like the show.

Because you couldn't just take anyone to *The Oprah Winfrey Show*. You took the person you loved the most—your mother, sister, best friend, daughter, son, husband, wife, coworker, or cousin. You took the person who stood by you in life. We called it your "top Oprah pick." When people got tickets to the show, they somehow found a way to afford the flights, hotels, babysitters, outfits, and pedicures, and that was never lost on me. It was never lost on anyone.

This is what made our audience unique and different from any other talk show audience. The energy of love pulsing from the people who not only stood next to one another at the show but also stood next to one another in life was extraordinary. That magic can only happen for one reason, and her name is Oprah.

You know who your top Oprah pick is. Spend more time with that person. *The Oprah Winfrey Show* doesn't have to be on the air for you to know who your top Oprah pick is. Make sure you let this person know how important he or she is to you.

I always asked people to literally turn to the person next to them and thank that person for being beside them. I encouraged people to say "thank you" and "I love you." One mom who was with her son thanked me after the show because her son said, "I love you, Mom," for the first time and she told me he would never have said those words if he hadn't been prompted to do so.

I remember a woman standing up in the back row of the studio during one of my warm-ups who said that her dream was to have coffee with Oprah. My team knew immediately what was coming next because they spoke *Sally Lou*.

"Can someone please go get a cup of coffee for this woman?" I asked. And with that, the woman—whose name I do not remember, unfortunately— drank her coffee in the back row of the audience and fulfilled her dream of having coffee with Oprah.

A story that will stay in my heart forever happened when my beautiful friend Jeanne brought her beautiful sister Jan to the show. *The Oprah Winfrey Show* was on Jan's bucket list, and Jan had just been diagnosed with melanoma. I arranged tickets for Jeanne and Jan, and they attended a show about chocolate. Most talk shows would have given a bag of chocolate as a parting gift to the audience. Our show's entire set was made out of chocolate, and the audience was invited to taste it.

I spent a lot of time with both sisters that day, and while my heart broke, it was also full as I watched these two sisters forget about Jan's diagnosis and have a sweet moment together. Jeanne and Jan will always remain in my heart, and I will always be grateful that I was able to provide a memory for them both to cherish. When Jan passed away, I know she took that sweet memory with her.

We received so many ticket requests from people who were facing the end of their lives, and I granted as many as I possibly could that came my way. I wasn't saving lives. I was making them better.

We also had a lot of fun. We had a dance party every day, we shared our hearts, and at the end of show day, I would peel off my cute outfit, take off my Prada show shoes, and change into my lululemons because I definitely needed an outfit change for everyone's sake.

In 2011, when the show was ending, my team and I went to see a show called *Oprah! Living Your Best Laugh* at the Annoyance Theater. The show started with a cast member doing the warm-up. We all realized it was a spoof of me, and I have to say that it was pretty funny. I kind of felt like I had made it.

Whenever people in our audience took the time to call or write to us to complain, I always took the time to call them back and listen. I knew it was impossible for everyone to feel like their experience was exactly what they had hoped for, but it killed me if anyone left the show disappointed. What I discovered is what Oprah taught the world, people just want to know they matter.

As soon as I took the time to listen to what someone had to say, not only did they feel better, I felt better too. I always learned something from the person I called that my team and I could do better. And I always put those lessons into play and promised the person I was speaking to that we would. That is how we ran our customer service at *The Oprah Winfrey Show*. Every person mattered. Their words mattered, and they were seen.

Whenever you have to have a tough conversation, always have that conversation in person or by phone. Don't be lazy and use text or email. Be human and speak, and then watch everything resolve itself right before your eyes.

I often wonder if the girl with the clipboard had this kind of connection with her *Mike Douglas* audience. Times were very different then, and certainly, Oprah drew this kind of love that no other human could. All I know is that when we use our talents in an environment we love, we open ourselves up to opportunities that can't even be described as work—unless you call it kingdom work.

Audiences are not reserved for television personalities, warm-up acts, or professional speakers. There is an audience for everyone—teachers, fitness instructors, coaches, doctors, lawyers, wellness coaches, rabbis, ministers, comedians, cashiers, chefs, influencers. Whatever your title is, there is an audience for you, so love the audience you have.

Whatever size your audience is, listen to them. Love your audience by connecting with them in your own unique way, and make the connection yours. And remember, they showed up to see *you*.

LOVESPEAKS LESSON #9: Be a good listener. As speakers, we think we have to do all the speaking. We worry so much about what we are going to say that we sometimes forget to consider what our audience might say.

When we listen to our audience, we are more present and able to weave in content our audience has shared with us. When people are heard, they connect with you on a whole new level. This is truly when love speaks.

Love your audience by listening to them, and let your audience know they matter. Whether you are a speaker, an influencer, a leader of a company or a nonprofit, a fan, a client, a customer, or an employee, you have an audience. There is an audience for everyone, and yours is waiting.

When was the last time you felt heard?

_____

_____

_____

LOVESPEAKS PRACTICE: Get to know and care for your most important audience—you. Take time to listen to yourself by practicing stillness. Take a walk alone without headphones and listen to the sounds that surround you. Take time for meditation.

ALTERNATIVE LOVESPEAKS PRACTICE: Take time to listen to someone with your full attention without speaking until they finish. Ask someone to listen to you. Let them know you only want to be heard, and ask them if they would be generous with their time and just listen.

LIVE LOVESPEAKS: Meet Maleesa. My friend Maleesa Xiong has made listening an art. A self-described creative doer and explorer and mother of three, Maleesa starts her story with "a lover of the not so obvious and creator of the not so complicated." What is obvious to me is that my friend Maleesa stops to listen to the world around her and to notice its beauty, which is why I would like to live inside her Instagram story because her daily life is simply beautiful.

She can walk down a beach and collect a handful of sea glass when most of us wouldn't see one piece. She discovers cool places, interesting people, and peaceful moments daily. She takes time to listen to the waves of Lake Michigan, and I'm certain she has a direct line to Mother Nature because beauty attracts beauty. All magic makers know that.

One day I was sitting on the beach at the lake and meditating, and Maleesa texted me. She told me she was listening to a podcast I was a guest on, and I told her I was listening to her podcast, the gentle waves of Lake Michigan.

Maleesa can make anything beautiful. We first met when our kids were in the middle school play. It was my first time as a theater mom, and I was enjoying the moment. I confidently walked in on opening night with my store-bought flowers and saw Maleesa was selling simple bouquets that were works of art and clearly made with love.

I ditched my store-bought flowers and purchased hers, and I was happy for the upgrade. That's what Maleesa does. She upgrades the not so obvious and makes beauty uncomplicated. Those are skills I wish I had.

Maleesa lost her husband at a very young age. She has raised her three children magnificently, and instead of seeing what they have lost, Maleesa only sees what they can find. She listens for what's next. She explores for new treasures. She collects beautiful things, and she discovers a world most of us never take the time to notice.

Everything about Maleesa feels uncomplicated because she moves through life with an ease that is lacking in most people. Maleesa is a reminder to take time to stop, look, listen, and discover; to not be ruled by our schedule or our to-do list; and to build a relationship with Mother Nature, a beautiful force we should all pay more attention to.

Who reminds you to listen and look for beauty in the not so obvious?

_____

_____

_____

CHAPTER 10

Does Anyone Even Like Me?

The most courageous act is still to think for yourself aloud.
—COCO CHANEL

We all want to be liked, especially today when likes can be turned into livelihoods. As a midlifer, we don't get a lot of likes. Midlife sometimes feels more like being ignored than being liked. So I try to turn everything into a party, no matter how mundane it is.

Like the time I took communion after not eating carbs or drinking wine for four months. My church serves fresh baked bread the first Sunday of the month, and lucky for me, it was a first Sunday. I sucked on that little morsel of bread and drop of wine like it was the best cocktail party I had ever been to. If there is ever a reason to celebrate Jesus, it is on the first Sunday of the month at my church.

One day I wet my pants in Walgreens. Yep, I full on wet my pants right there on the corner of happy and healthy! Thankfully, I was wearing my black lululemon pants, so there was no evidence. But I was completely embarrassed. That was the day my bladder therapy party started. I called my doctor and signed up.

I thought bladder therapy was going to be on a treadmill, which shows you how much I know about bladder therapy. For eight straight weeks, I went to bladder therapy, and let's just say there was no treadmill. My therapist Katie was young, smart, and adorable, and I asked her over and over again why the hell she chose this profession. It was clear Katie loved bladder PT as much as I loved television, proving there are careers out there for all of us to love.

Katie explained every nuance of my internal system like I would tell you about an episode of *Friends*. In return, I made Katie laugh at each visit with my *Living Loveman* content because even if you have your arm in my bladder for forty-five minutes, I'm still going to make you laugh.

Along with wetting your pants, menopause definitely keeps people from liking you. It's hard enough to like yourself in menopause, let alone expect someone else to. I don't know when menopause began for me, but I know that I am not through it yet. I can only describe menopause as what it must feel like to be swallowed alive by a dragon.

Speaking of heat, the day we shot the back cover of this book, it was 100 degrees in Chicago. We considered rescheduling, but then I thought, *If I can manage menopause, I can manage record-high temperatures in a pantsuit and heels.*

My husband lugged the *Oprah* audience seat to the beach from his car, which served as my green room, and I got stung by a bee on my foot. Sweat was pouring down my entire body, but luckily, I was prepared because I brought a bottle of Dom Pérignon to stay *hydrated*, which meant I had a Yeti filled with ice. I stuck my foot in the Yeti and managed to take down the swelling of my beesting. The Dom helped with the pain as well.

I am always prepared to use humor, alcohol, or honesty to make people like me, and I am grateful I have lived three-quarters of my life with authentic, face-to-face likes. I worry that social media has replaced the real stuff people have enjoyed for centuries. It can be exhausting and take us away from what matters most. It's a second job and a slippery slope.

Admittedly, I am a number-one offender and user because I love the immediacy of it as well as the production and connection value. I have to take breaks because it can suck me in and waste hours of my day, not to mention keep me from staying in the moment with the people who are front row in my life.

As *The Oprah Winfrey Show* was ending, I passed Oprah in the hallway, and she asked me how I was doing. I answered, "Will people even like me when the show is over?" The words just came tumbling out of my mouth. I wasn't being dramatic. I just wasn't using a filter. And like usual, I would find that our words have power.

When you have a successful brand behind you, people like you more, call you more, and invite you out more. People like me less now, but the people who like me legitimately like me, and that feels good.

During *The Oprah Winfrey Show* years, I remember being at a party with my family. My sisters and I were standing together when a woman came up to us and said, "Which one is the sister who works for Oprah?" Meanwhile, my sister Cindy had made millions as an investment banker on Wall Street and my sister Susan, the physician's assistant, had reinvented her career by using her medical training to defend doctors as a researcher for a law firm. But this woman wanted to talk to the sister who worked for Oprah. I wonder if she would want to talk to me now.

Without the brand, there is more silence, and as we already know, silence kills momentum and builds fear. Add midlife to the mix, and suddenly, I find myself with less noise and feeling a bit lonely. My kids are grown and out of the house. I no longer work with a team. Rejections are more common, and as a midlifer, we are losing our parents. Life gets quiet. I grew up in a house with lots of noise, so a quiet house is new for me.

I don't operate well in quiet, except when I am in meditation. I continue to learn to watch what I say, but with my mouth, it's hard. Good things are great to put in the universe, but when we say things like "Will people even like me?" sometimes those things happen because of the power and energy we attach to our words. So I try to only put good things into the universe. I try to love speak 24/7. But the founder of lovespeaks is human too!

Before we were married, my husband got courtside tickets to a Bulls game through a family friend. It was the late '80s (best decade ever), and the Chicago Bulls were hot. I said to my husband, "If Michael Jordan touches me tonight, I will lose my mind."

Michael Jordan didn't just touch me. He literally fell into my lap. Out of all the laps he could have fallen into on his breakaway, he fell into mine. I will never forget when Air Jordan lifted his head from my lap, smiled, and said, "Sorry!"

As promised, I lost my mind, and so did everyone around me. I swore I would never again wash the Guess jeans I was wearing. I have no idea where they are now, but I should have framed them.

When I recovered from my "meet cute" with Michael Jordan, I left my seat to call my dad to tell him the news, and even though he could barely hear me over the noise of the stadium, he knew another Lulu story was in the books.

I'm an Aquarian, which means I am a dreamer, a bit eccentric, an emotional person, and a deep thinker. I have a lot of trouble turning my brain off, and meditation has made my creative juices flow even stronger.

I used to be a varsity sleeper. Now I can't sleep because I'm dreaming of everything I want to accomplish.

I hear the clock ticking. I want to produce the podcast I wrote years ago. I want to perform my stand-up act. I dream of show pitches and write business ideas in the middle of the night. I wanted this book. I want more books. I want to create online coursework for speaking and healing. I want to become a Reiki master. I want my master's degree in psychology. I want to do transformational makeovers. It never stops, which means this midlifer will never stop trying.

But in midlife I have been turned down more than I'd like to admit—probably because I have the guts to audition or apply for anything, one of the perks of being older. I have learned to develop a thick skin, but I'm not going to lie. It's hard. Our egos are at stake, and our happiness is too, not to mention our livelihoods.

I auditioned to be the warm-up act for a professional sports team, and while I was waiting in the lobby for my name to be called, I noticed everyone around me was twenty-something. It didn't even dawn on me until I left the building and never heard from them again.

I turned Johnny Cash's "Ring of Fire" into a song specifically for the team, and while I was performing my act, the young producer I was auditioning for started to laugh so hard that I decided to laugh too. What other choice did I have? Laughter is not only my exit plan. It's my only plan.

I have applied to TEDx, called on corporations that care to speak to their employees, met with speaker bookers, and also applied to the Obama Foundation, a Democratic candidate's campaign, a successful online women's platform, a nonprofit benefiting women and children, a new talk show that literally screams my name, and at fifty-six years old, I went to New York City for a casting call to be an ambassador for a major brand.

A resounding no was heard. Is it my age? Maybe. Is it that I'm not attached to a big brand? Maybe. Is it because someone didn't like me? I hope not. Hearing someone say no always stings no matter what age we are, but the noes always make us hungrier for yeses. Sometimes we have to create our own yeses, which is what I have chosen to do. While I have been blessed with many yeses and don't need anyone to feel sorry for me, I can tell you the noes in midlife hurt.

That is what motivated me to write this book. Sometimes we have to create our own content. If we aren't getting the yeses we want, we have to create our own. No one can tell you no when the content is yours. I have always wanted to be an author, and thanks to me, I now get to change my category on Instagram from motivational speaker, a title I don't love, to author. If you want to change your category, do it yourself. Don't wait for someone to do it for you.

When you roll with excitement full-time, it's hard to live without it. It's like having great sex and then not having great sex. But at least you had it, right? So that's where I operate from now. I had it (an exciting career) and still do. It's just not as loud as it once was. I have also had great sex—if anyone is wondering.

Turn up the volume in your life by staying connected to the people who like you. Start a text thread with people who like you. Name it, and use it. My family has an "Oaks Women" text thread that includes my sisters, my nieces, my daughters, and my mom. We cover topics ranging from IUDs to recipes and everything in between. Nothing is off-limits.

Sometimes it moves faster than Twitter, and I really don't even need to read theSkimm because I get my news from this thread. But most of all, I get the laughter that I crave and the connection that defines me.

When I was the keynote speaker at Lafayette College's Council of Lafayette Women Conference, I suggested that before everyone left campus, they start a text thread with their fellow alums to keep the connection they were feeling in the moment close to them always. Start yours if you don't have one already. Connection helps keep our lives loud. Get your silence through meditation.

Years ago a women I didn't know said to me, "Aren't you the Oprah lady who always has her house on the market?" In my mind I was like, *Is that what people think of me?* This was before the show ended and before I even had time to consider whether people liked me or not. It was also around the time our mortgage was strangling us. Her comment stuck with me for years, and at the time I was offended. Today I appreciate her honesty.

Even though this woman was labeling me just like Mrs. Thompson did, I welcome her honesty now. I take honesty over silence any day of the week.

She was right. I was the Oprah lady who always had her house on the market. It just wasn't the nicest way to say it.

I have learned in midlife to surround myself with people who like me and tell me the truth. I would suggest that for anyone at any stage of life. The lesson I think we can all take away is when we truly like ourselves, we attract people into our lives who truly like us and love us. Midlife shouldn't have to wake us up to know this. But sometimes lessons come late in life. And that's okay too.

LOVESPEAKS LESSON #10: Love your people. I appreciate the people who have stuck with me through my business and through midlife and have loved me and liked me for all the right reasons. I appreciate all the new people I have met through my new world as an entrepreneur, I call them my lovespeaks peeps!

Don't ever let someone tell you that you are not enough. We are all enough. And we all deserve to honestly live our lives with the freedom to be who we are and share who we are at any age. To my midlife friends, don't ever stop going after your dreams. To my millennial friends, you will be midlifers too one day, so welcome in the wisdom from us midlifers as we welcome your incredible talents into our world.

We can't do it alone. We need one another. In order to be more efficient, midlifers need millennials. In order to be more focused, millennials need midlifers. If you don't have your midlifer or millennial mate, find one. It's a must.

As midlifers, we have earned the right to say what we want, and we've also earned the right to let some things go if those things no longer serve us. We have earned the right to laugh our asses off at ourselves and with one another. I have found this is to be a much happier way to live life.

Write your dream here, and direct message me when it happens

_____

_____

_____

LOVESPEAKS PRACTICE: Spend more time with people who genuinely like you and those you genuinely like. Hold onto that good energy, and bring that good energy into other areas of your life where it's needed. Don't waste your precious time with people who don't want the best for you. That energy has no place in a world where love speaks.

Midlifers, please make friends with millennials, and millennials, please make friends with midlifers. Millennials think differently than midlifers, and we can both benefit from each other's way of thinking.

My must-have millennial and brand genius, Aly Nauta, has taught me so much about social media and branding. I move at about a tenth of her speed. What takes me thirty minutes to post takes Aly three minutes, but I get there eventually. Remember baby steps. We don't all move forward at the same pace. I think of it like yoga. When I first started my yoga practice, I could basically do child's pose. Now I can do bakasana, otherwise known as crow pose. Baby steps.

Remember to fill up your life with people who don't think like you, look like you, or act like you but who genuinely like you.

ALTERNATIVE LOVESPEAKS PRACTICE: Remind yourself daily of why you like who you are.

LIVE LOVESPEAKS: Meet Rita. My friend Rita Coburn, a mother of two, is a creator, director, writer, speaker, and founder of RCW Media Productions, Inc. Rita starts her story by saying, "I put my eggs in one basket because my basket's good." Rita is one of the most confident women I know and also a dear friend. When I look at Rita, I see all the women who have come before her and all the women who will come after her. Rita is a woman of many stories.

I met Rita in the early 1990s when we worked together at a talk show (the other show I quit). After working a twelve- to fifteen-hour day together, we would each drive home and pick up our house phones in our bedrooms and talk for another two hours. This was before we all had cell phones and people actually picked up the phone to talk to one another, even after spending the entire day together. We never ran out of things to say, and we still don't. I will always prefer a Rita conversation over a Rita text because no one delivers a line like Rita.

In 2006, we were reunited at Harpo Studios when Rita joined the Harpo Radio team as Maya Angelou's XM Radio producer. One sunny afternoon we were sitting outside the studio, having lunch at the Harpo café, and talking about how Rita was the perfect person to tell Maya Angelou's story. We talked about how this generation of elders was going to be gone soon and how she could bring their stories to life, especially Dr. Angelou's. In 2017, Rita produced and codirected *Still I Rise*, a magnificent documentary film and winner of a Peabody, which tells Dr. Angelou's story.

There is no one I know who loves her basket more than Rita, which is why I love having her in my life. She is a reminder to love my basket too and not to worry whether or not anyone else does. There is no stopping Rita Coburn. Age will never be a factor for her dreams, only a motivation to do more. If you want to love your basket more deeply, watch *Still I Rise*, and remember what a privilege it is to be a woman at every age.

A great reminder for me was when I was a guest on Gayle King's former show on OWN the day after we taped *Oprah's Surprise Spectacular*. Gayle said to me, "It's not over for you, Sally Lou."

And I responded, "It's not?" Because I actually thought it was.

Gayle's words were an invitation to me to believe there was more, and so there is. Women supporting women is the greatest gift we can give one another. Always remember your words have power. Speak up, empower others, and thank the people who support you along the way. Thank you, Gayle King!

How do you remind yourself it's not over?

_____

_____

_____

CHAPTER 11

Faith Is Cheaper than Botox

*In a culture of scarcity and perfectionism, there's a surprisingly simple
reason we want to own, integrate, and share our stories of struggle.
We do this because we feel the most alive when we're connecting
with others and being brave with our stories—it's in our biology.*
—BRENÉ BROWN

Brené Brown's books, my faith, Botox, and Beyoncé were key factors
in getting me through my next chapter. I was guilty of putting
my career ahead of my marriage during *The Oprah Winfrey Show*
years, and when the show ended, it caught up with me. I took my
eye off my marriage, and it fell prey to some trouble. As promised, *Living
Loveman* has a chapter I struggle with.

Trouble is code for anything you want it to be. I give you the freedom
to fill in the blank. If you are wondering why I am skirting the issue, my
answer is one word—children. I have them, and no matter what their age
(mine happen to be adults), mothers do everything they can to protect their
children.

My immediate solution to my trouble was Botox. I sold my Lollapalooza
tickets for a small profit and used the cash to get Botox. For those of you who
don't live in Chicago and aren't ages fifteen to twenty-one, Lollapalooza is
a four-day music festival where girls wear tube tops and boys wear no tops.
It's a super hard ticket to get, and yes, selling my greatest asset for Botox felt
like a powerful transaction.

It's impossible to talk about midlife without talking about Botox. It
fills in the lines of my middle-aged face, and I have been known to get an
injection or two. I was hoping Botox would make me look younger, and like
usual, even in my worst hour, I was cracking jokes.

I sat down in the plastic surgeon's chair, having never met her before, and I told her my story. I made her laugh so hard that she was having trouble keeping the needle steady. That's me, always looking for the joke, especially when I am in pain. I see every chair I sit in as an invitation for therapy and a new audience.

Dr. Love (which is code for my adoration) told me I reminded her of Jenny McCarthy. Clearly, Botox isn't that good, but it sure felt nice to be put in the same category as a Playmate of the Year, even though I'm pretty sure Dr. Love was referring to funny Jenny, not bunny Jenny.

But hey, I was willing to take any version of Jenny Dr. Love was throwing my way. I happen to love Jenny McCarthy because she is funny, bawdy, and totally overshares like I do. Plus she's married to Donnie Wahlberg. Let's just say producing the *New Kids on the Block* show in 1989 was the only show I ever produced that rated well, and Donnie Wahlberg will always rate number one with me.

But Botox couldn't fill the hole in my heart or turn me into a *Playboy* bunny. I was struggling with something way bigger, so I went to church. And that's when I realized my best friend Faith had way more to offer me than Botox ever could, and she was a much more affordable plan to getting my life back because faith is cheaper than Botox.

I am lucky to have a lot of friends, but when shit hits the fan, Faith is my go-to girl. You can call her God, Spirit, Source, Mother Nature, or a knowing. Call her what you want. Just call her because if you don't have a relationship with your BFF, your "best friend faith," midlife can get rough.

The week before my unexpected Botox appointment, I stood in Oprah Winfrey's office and quit my job. I said to my boss, "As your esteemed student, I am ready to fly on my own." I was ready to start my own business and continue to do what I loved, connecting audiences to a brand. *The Oprah Winfrey Show* stage was no longer an option for me, and I wanted to find work that would move my heart like her stage had.

We hugged. I cried, and we said goodbye. It was beautiful.

We've all heard the saying, "If you want to make God laugh, tell him about your plans." I was about to learn this lesson the hard way. Within ten minutes of walking out of Oprah Winfrey's office, I discovered my marriage was in trouble.

My big lesson: Never tell Oprah your plans. Let her tell you what your plan is. She's Oprah! Ever since I left *The Oprah Winfrey Show*, it feels like my life has become a talk show. My joke is I want to start a podcast called *Living Your Worst Life* because life is better with Oprah.

Before my fifties, the only thing I had lost, with the exception of my grandparents and my uncle Jody, who all died at appropriate ages, were my two front teeth. I broke them off in the fifth grade trying to beat a boy in a relay race in gym class.

I had a marriage of twenty-three years to my best friend, a loving family, three magnificent children, a beautiful home, a dream job with Oprah, the best of friends, and an extended family without one bad apple on either side. When it comes to family, my husband and I both hit the jackpot.

Enter my fiftieth, and *whoosh*, there goes my house, potentially my marriage, my job, my dad, my dog, some friends, and eight more teeth. I take really good care of my teeth by the way, but if you add stress to my original injury in fifth grade along with some bad genetics, I seem to spend more time in the dentist chair than I do in the therapy chair. Try starting a speaking business without teeth. It's not easy.

One thing I didn't mind losing was weight. My ass had never looked so cute. Weight loss experts must study women in my condition because I was doing everything every dieter has ever done, from not eating to popping pills to throwing up and overexercising. It wasn't exactly the healthiest routine, but I was skinny.

What I went through is called life, and luckily, I am still here to work out the tough stuff. That's one thing we can always count on. There will always be tough stuff. Trust me when I say I have perspective. I really do. My prayer list for families who have lost children is too long, and every day when I pray for them, I pray that God grants these families moments of peace. And I thank God for mine.

And while I would never recommend the journey I took, I will always recommend the faith I found. When life suddenly takes away what you thought was yours, it becomes very black and white. There is absolutely no gray. You fight for what's yours—your dignity, your truth, your family, your marriage. Faith makes the fight easier because faith reminds us that Sunday's coming. In other words, we can always start over.

Most people would never share the shitty parts of their stories, but the shitty parts are what build us into much less shitty people. It is truly when love speaks. When I share my story in more detail with women who have earned the right to hear it, they lean in closer. That's how I know my story benefits others. One day I will write about it. For now it lives in my stand-up act.

I share this part of my story for women who are having a hard time smiling or laughing, for women who are in the midst of healing and working hard to make their marriage work with no guarantee, and for women who have chosen divorce as their way of healing because there is absolutely nothing wrong with divorce. Sometimes it's not only the best option. It's the only option.

My husband and I chose to stay together because we were both willing and committed to the healing work. That's when darkness becomes light. And at the center of that light is my girl Faith. This wasn't supposed to happen to me. Or maybe it was? As Voltaire says, "Faith consists in believing what reason cannot."

I was raised really well. Growing up, my parents taught me that truth is the only option, and for me, truth is always my road to healing. So many women live in silence. They may not have my stamina, confidence, education, faith, or support. I think about that a lot. I am privileged to have these things, and I do not take them for granted ever. We all want healing just like we all want purpose. And like purpose, we don't all heal at the same pace.

A year before my trouble, we were at Christmas Eve dinner, and I asked my family, "What would you do if you knew you couldn't fail?" My answer was to be stand-up comic. And then I said these words: "But I don't have enough pain." I went ahead and said *that*, knowing full well the power of our words. I opened the door and invited pain in.

We all have pain. We just have different levels of pain. And while our stories are never the same, we can always take a piece from someone else's story to help us with our own, which ultimately helps us with healing.

The piece of my story that is universal to anyone's pain is that we always know when a relationship is worth fighting for and when it is not, even with all of its flaws. Our relationships are never perfect. We all wear some scars, but we all know if the scars are worth the work. Sometimes my tears are actually tears of gratitude. Don't misunderstand me. There is pain in the tears, but I am also grateful for the strength of my faith. I'm so grateful it often makes me cry.

Don't waste your time when you know the relationship is not worth fighting for and fight for it when you know it is. Both parties have to be willing to do the work. If one door is closed, the work will never be successful. Even with two open doors, the work won't always be smooth. Setbacks are guaranteed. If the setback moves you forward, the work is always worthwhile.

As I began to pick up the broken pieces of my life after discovering my trouble, I went back to Harpo and asked for my job back. It was one of the hardest things I have ever had to do. I was ashamed, embarrassed, and terrified. That's when my boss—let's call her Heart—said four words that would give me hope and change my life. She said, "We've got your back." Those four words were proof that Oprah Winfrey, her producers, and her executive team didn't just put a brand of love on television. They lived that brand.

I had worked for this talk show for more than twenty years. I grew up on the set. And suddenly, I could have been a segment-one guest. The talk show producer had become a talk show guest overnight, and in that moment, my boss, who gave me her heart, a person I will forever love so deeply, gave me hope, security, and the strength to fight for my life back.

The building that had saved so many people's lives was saving mine. I was reminded that a woman-led company whose mission is to help you live your best life wasn't just a television show. It was a movement. I was part of the movement, and I was proud.

Many of us have had a moment in our lives when a woman says a few words that change our life. She could be a total stranger, a boss, or a best friend. This was my moment, and I will forever be in deep gratitude to my bighearted woman boss as well as the women who ran Oprah's company, starting with Oprah.

I was back at work, though barely, and guess who the universe delivered? My speaker hero Brené Brown arrived. I was assigned to work on researcher and storyteller Brené Brown's show for *Oprah's Lifeclass*, one of the last few shows we would produce with an audience.

As research, I started to read Brené Brown's book *Daring Greatly*, and instantly, I found that just like my friend Faith, this book was going to help save me too. Brené Brown writes about vulnerability, something I needed to be more of in my marriage, and shame, something my husband had been suffering from. Her words felt like they had been written for us. As we each read the book individually, we shared her lessons together, and this was the beginning of our healing.

Faith comes in all shapes and sizes. There are so many players on my faith team, many of whom have no idea who I am, including Brené Brown. I always say the three Bs saved me—Brené, Brown, and Beyoncé. I listened to Beyoncé's "Broken-Hearted Girl" and "Best Thing I Never Had" on repeat during many runs (before *Lemonade*).

On the day Brené Brown was a guest on *Oprah's Lifeclass*, I was more excited to meet Brené Brown than I was when I met Beyoncé. And trust me—I love Beyoncé. Nothing screams midlife more than wanting to meet a researcher who studies vulnerability and shame instead of a popstar who, at this writing, has 135 million followers on Instagram ... and growing.

When the *Lifeclass* show ended, I walked through the front entrance of our studio and saw Brené Brown standing with a producer. In that moment my eyes locked with hers and then she spoke to me and said, "You have great hair." But all I heard was, "You're doing great, Sally Lou," giving a whole new meaning to a good hair day.

My eyes filled with tears, and I quietly said, "Thank you. Your book helped save my marriage." I think she understood. And that's the cool thing about faith. Sometimes our faith players have no idea how integral their existence means to another person.

A few years later, I saw Brené Brown speak at the Ninety-Second Street Young Men's and Young Women's Hebrew Association, otherwise known as the Ninety-Second Street Y, while I was working in New York City. She told a story about how Maya Angelou was basically her faith player and how Maya Angelou had no idea. Her story reminded me that no matter who we are, we are all looking to be inspired by someone who leads us to work harder, heal faster, make better choices, and live in our truth.

Before I even got myself to church after I discovered my marriage trouble, my faith was already kicking in ... in both big and small ways. It started with sailboats. I was on a run to the beach, and when I reached Lake Michigan, I saw five sunfish sailboats out on the water. It was really early in the morning, and everything was still and quiet, except for these boats. I stopped at the edge of the pier and watched them. Suddenly, I saw them all capsize together and all rise back up together. Again, they capsized together, and they came up again together.

It dawned on me that this must be a sailing class, but the most magnificent message hit me so hard in my chest that I knew it was coming straight from my friend Faith. The sailboats were telling me that my family of five would rise again, that we would stay together, and that it would all be okay. We would have to do the work together, train hard, and learn from practice. It wasn't going to be easy. There would be times we would fall, but it would be worth it if we were willing to do the work. This was our own life class—a lesson that life is all about learning and that sometimes the lessons are staring us right in the face.

I also remember the rain. During those early weeks of discovering my trouble, the rain wouldn't stop. Sheets of rain pouring down, cracks of lightning, dark skies, and rumbling thunder. This went on for days after I saw the sailboats, and I couldn't help but think that maybe it was a clearing for a new beginning, almost like a sage smudge stick being waved across the sky. I could feel nature and the heavens speaking to me. I listened, and I felt a kind of comfort that is impossible to describe.

My husband and I met when we were twenty-two. He was one of two people my college roommate and best friend Andrea suggested I meet when I moved to Chicago for my television job. Andrea met my husband in London on the semester abroad my father wouldn't let me go on. The universe was now ready for me to meet my future husband.

SPEAK

The other person Andrea suggested I meet was her friend Henry. Andrea and Henry met when she spent a summer studying at Northwestern University. Henry became my first roommate in Chicago, and he is still one of my dearest friends. My ten boxes of clothes arrived in Chicago before I did, and Henry brought each one of them to my room. He met my wardrobe before he met me, and he still somehow loves me.

Henry's girlfriend, Marcy, who got my resume to *The Oprah Winfrey Show*, lived ten floors above us, and we immediately became friends. Today, Andrea, Henry, and Marcy are part of our support team, and so is Andrea's husband Pete. Pete was my college boyfriend, and I will try to explain this in the most uncomplicated way. I married my husband, whom Andrea met in London (during the semester I wanted to go on). Andrea married Pete, whom she met when he was my boyfriend in college, and Marcy married Henry, whom I lived with in Chicago. We all attended one another's weddings, and our stories are better than any reality show.

Marcy and Henry later divorced but remain the best of friends. You can find us getting together at Henry's Fire Island beachfront home, which he shares with his husband, Bob, laughing our asses off. We all love Bob the most, and he has to think we are crazy, which is why if we actually had a reality show, it would be titled *Make Room for Bob*. The content is endless.

People still talk about our wedding. We have a very close family and strong circle of friends, and my mom went overboard on everything. We didn't get married in a church because my husband is Jewish, which explains why my children are Jewish if you were wondering. While my mom had no idea what a chuppah was, she managed to create the most magnificent chuppah ever made.

The only rabbi in the Philadelphia area who would participate in an interfaith wedding at the time was already booked. Somehow my mother convinced him to officiate our wedding. He nicknamed my mom "Percy" for her unending perseverance. We only knew this man for a day and a half, and we still send him a holiday card every year because he impacted our hearts immediately.

Oprah was there. She surprised me. I literally almost fell over in my Carolina Herrera dress when I was walking down the aisle and saw Oprah Winfrey sitting next to my friends. My knees buckled, and my dad held me up to keep me from face-planting.

I still think about Oprah's decision to get on a plane to witness our vows, and I can hardly believe the generosity it took for her to give us her precious time. Her presence at our wedding serves as a reminder to me to work on my marriage the way I worked on her show. And I expect the same from my husband.

We raised our children in the Jewish faith because I knew it would be hard for my husband to raise our children Christian. I wrote and produced each bar and bat mitzvah service for our children and tutored my in-laws on how to pronounce the Hebrew prayers. I have zero regrets. I loved every second of it and am so proud of my children's Jewish faith.

When I was thirteen, I went to a bar or bat mitzvah every weekend and helped my friends study. I wore the same outfit to almost every party, and yes, I still have it as it is part of my Sally Lou Oaks Important Outfit Collection. My husband attended his first bat mitzvah service when he was forty years old and wasn't a bar mitzvah until he was forty-four. It seems we were living in each other's worlds before our worlds came together.

Being under the chuppah at our wedding and being surrounded by our family and bridal party was the most inclusive feeling, and in that moment I knew we would raise our future children Jewish. It was my decision, not my husband's, and he was grateful.

A few months after our daughter Marin's bat mitzvah, we were at Christmas dinner, and my father said that Marin's bat mitzvah was the single greatest family event we had ever experienced together. And trust me—we have had some pretty fabulous celebrations. I loved that my dad could fully embrace my decision to raise our children in the Jewish faith because my vote is always for inclusive.

We try to spend as much time as we can in temple and in church and of course, in therapy, which is what continues to help us. Our rabbi, minister, therapists, energy healer, and family are our key players on our healing team. We take faith and healing any way we can get it because we need it.

When I turned fifty and received my American Association of Retired Persons card in the mail, otherwise known as AARP, the conversation suddenly changed from "Who's in the studio with Oprah today?" to "Your colonoscopy report came back, and you'll need to return in three years, not ten." That's not sexy.

But you know what is? Truth. Truth is sexy. Truth is freedom. Truth is intimate. I started to tell the truth too. I owned my horrible relationship with money. It made my husband less fearful of me, and today our partnership is better for it. If you are keeping the truth from someone, you can't be intimate with them, and you can't grow with them. That is no way to live. Truth is all we can ask for to live a healthy life.

Like so many couples, my husband and I are far from perfect. But we are committed to the work, and we continue to be a work in progress. The love we share for each other is undeniable. Lucky for me I like to work, and lucky for me, I also like me.

J. R. R, Tolkien says, "Faithless is he [or in my case, she] that says farewell when the road darkens."

LOVESPEAKS LESSON #11: Truth literally sets us free. The pain we suffer when we keep secrets is debilitating. It brings destruction to our lives. When you speak with your partner, your family, your friends, your coworkers, or an audience, tell the truth. We lose nothing when we tell the truth. We lose everything when we don't.

Is there a truth you need to tell someone or yourself?

_____

_____

_____

LOVESPEAKS PRACTICE: When you feel trapped and like you can't speak your truth, look for an open door that will lead you to a better option. Look for the exits. No one ever has to suffer alone. Set yourself free by speaking your truth. There are so many open doors to a life led by truth. You just have to know where to find the openings.

The option to keep the truth from someone you love, your partner, your audience, a coworker, or a friend should never be the door you choose. That door is a closed door. The truth is always through an open door.

ALTERNATIVE LOVESPEAKS PRACTICE: If you are keeping the truth from someone, consult with a professional who can help you.

LIVE LOVESPEAKS: Our holistic therapy team and energy healer help us grow and have been gifts from God. Our holistic marriage therapist brings in spiritual practices to our healing, and our energy healer helps us shed emotional pain from our physical bodies. We are committed to healing both physically and spiritually.

We work really hard. I get frustrated that it takes my husband longer to get to the bottom of his pain because I happen to be so good at therapy. It's suddenly my new talent. But I have learned the road is long, and as long as the person you're riding with is working, then riding together is worth it.

When I first met with our energy healer, she told me that I would have the greatest intimacy with my husband that I have ever had. I told her that wasn't possible because I had way too much pain. She said, "When two people tell the truth into me, you see." Then she tapped on my chest and said again, "Into me, you see. Into me, you see. Intimacy." And then I got it.

And she was right. Once the truth was told and we made the decision to heal, our hearts connected so strongly, which made room for intimacy. Like I said, you can't be intimate with someone who is keeping something from you. It's impossible.

My husband is a cancer survivor. I discovered a tumor on his testicle just after we had our daughter Carly. He knew it was there, but he told me he thought it would go away. I made him go to the doctor immediately, and he was diagnosed with testicular cancer. Today he is a twenty-three-year cancer survivor, and we celebrate every year he has been given.

Bad things don't go away. They fester. They grow. They become cancer. Don't forget to tell yourself the truth too.

How do you keep your door open?

_____

_____

_____

CHAPTER 12

The Unexpected Thank-You

We have to be better. We have to love more, hate less.
—MEGAN RAPINOE, US WOMEN'S SOCCER STAR

The world seems so split lately and somewhat unforgiving. People seem more comfortable being divided than united. Sadly, it's easier to be divided. It takes less work to hate and way more work to love, to heal, to listen, and to forgive. That's why love always wins. It's because love takes work.

I wasn't looking for a lesson in forgiveness. I thought I already knew everything there was to know about it, being raised by parents who led by example and working for *The Oprah Winfrey Show*. I already understood that forgiveness is not about accepting what someone did as okay. It's about letting go so that the past does not hold us prisoner.

But lessons are often unexpected. I had to do a whole lot of soul searching to truly understand why forgiveness was not only my best option but really my only option. I don't think I ever felt more powerful than during this period of healing. I felt like a superwoman. Everything I said was heard. Everything I wanted I got. I was lean and mean. I didn't do one thing that didn't serve me. I protected my children like a mama bear protects her cubs. I was strong, and I was mighty.

The hardest part of healing is holding on to that power as time marches on. We get lazy and think we've done the work, and it will all be okay. It's not okay. Healing is a full-time job with no days off, no comp time, and no vacation days.

I got a tattoo to remind myself of my strength, to work hard, and to remember I am loved. I asked my godsister Amy, who is a talented graphic artist, to sketch my tattoo for me. Amy is my graphic designer for my business and this book, and she is like a sister to me. My tattoo is a red heart inside an O. It represents my Oaks family circle, which protects my heart.

Amy's sketch looks nothing like the O of Oprah's logo, but my tattoo sure does. I guess I didn't really research the best tattoo artist. When people assume the O is for Oprah, I have to explain my maiden name so people don't think I'm crazy. It turns out that I'm okay with the unexpected meaning too.

There are days when I totally get the work my husband and I are doing is soulful and filled with purpose, and there are days when I think there is nothing soulful at all about our work. That's why it's called work. In one session our therapist, whom I call Dr. God, led us in an exercise that changed everything for me. He asked my husband to look at me and say, "This will never happen again." So my husband said, "This will never happen again." Okay, great! It will never happen again! How easy is that? I wasn't buying it.

What our therapist did next changed everything for me. He asked my husband to add, "If I want out of our marriage, you will be the first to know." This was a statement I could trust. No one can say their marriage will last forever, but anyone can agree to tell their partner first before there is trouble.

If I could go back to this session, I would have asked our therapist to add, "I will never keep anything from you no matter how deep my pain is." Note to self. Note to all. When pain isn't healed, it shows up in other ways.

Like I said, I would never recommend the journey, but the journey woke me up. And in a very real and unexpected way, part of me felt like someone needed to be thanked because, as you know I am a fan of the thank-you note. But I don't think Emily Post would approve of mine. I will leave it for the comedy stage.

I can't plan for triggers. They come without warning. They are hard to explain, but if you have been through some pain, you know what I'm talking about. It could simply be a name, a phrase, a song, or a location. It could be anything that is a reminder of the circumstances affiliated with your pain. Getting through the triggers with dignity and truth is the goal.

My husband and I speak in compound sentences, which we learned in therapy, and this is the single greatest road to healing. A compound sentence is a sentence with more than one subject. The first part of the sentence acknowledges why the person you are speaking to has the right to have pain, and the second part is what the person who is speaking is requesting.

For example, my husband could say, "Sally Lou, I know I have caused you pain, and I am sorry for that, but I need you to understand I have feelings too. Can you please give me some time to hear them?" This takes years of training. Trust me. And the practice is definitely easier for women than for men. At least it is in my house. But I highly recommend this language because it can save a marriage, a friendship, or any relationship you are struggling with.

Trust me when I tell you that I am not perfect. I know what shame feels like. In the height of dealing with my own demons, I had a Neiman Marcus bill I was not proud of. I lived that lie. It was awful. We are human. We make mistakes. We get back up again when we fall, and we do the work.

I have also learned that women build fences and men build containers. Women build fences to keep outside temptations at bay, whereas men build containers to stuff things in they don't want to face. Admittedly, this is my own finding through the work my husband and I have done, but if you think about it, it makes sense.

There will always be mistakes. Telling the truth and doing the work is the only way out of a mistake. Just like the mistakes we make when we speak, it's what we do with our mistakes that our audience remembers, and it's what we do with our mistakes that our loved ones remember.

The core of my business I was about to build before quitting my dream job at *The Oprah Winfrey Show* was about letting love speak. I had no idea at the time that it would be me who would be doing the work, learning how to truly let love speak. But that's what happens when we think we know our plan and realize we don't. God was laughing, so I decided to laugh too.

LOVESPEAKS LESSON #12: An unknown author says, "Forgiveness doesn't excuse their behavior. Forgiveness prevents their behavior from destroying your heart." Forgiving doesn't mean forgetting. Nor does it mean that what someone did was okay. It means that you've let go of the anger and guilt that keeps you prisoner.

Forgiveness is the greatest gift you can give yourself. It is a gift of self-love. It's a gift that allows you to keep being who you are without having to give up a piece of your identity. Being yourself is one of the single greatest assets a person can have—as a human, a partner, a boss, a friend, a parent, and also a speaker. Even through all the pain I have experienced, I'm still me.

Is there someone you need to forgive?

_____

_____

LOVESPEAKS PRACTICE: Everyone has a story. If people in your life have brought you pain, consider their stories too. If these people mean anything to you, ask them where their pain is coming from and how you can help support them. When you see people acting out of character, it is a sign they need help. I know this firsthand. I also know when you help loved ones discover the source of their pain, love follows.

If the pain is coming from a stranger, release that person from your life because he or she means nothing to you, and take care of yourself. Do the work that nourishes and serves you.

ALTERNATIVE LOVESPEAKS PRACTICE: If forgiving someone in person is too hard for you, speak to the individuals as if he or she were standing beside you. Forgive the person. Release him or her. And stop being the person's prisoner. I have done this, and it is a beautiful gift to give yourself.

LIVE LOVESPEAKS: Holding hate keeps darkness in our lives. The only way out of the dark and into the light is through forgiveness. Sometimes the person we struggle with forgiving the most is ourselves.

If you are someone who is struggling, remember that tomorrow is coming. That is why we are here. We can always start over.

Find support. Find a way out. Find the light. Find an open door. Truth is always our best option.

I avoided a difficult conversation with a friend. I knew something was wrong, but I didn't have the courage to ask why. I worked for more than a year in therapy to have the conversation, and when I was finally brave enough to have it, I found something out that could have resolved my pain as well as my friend's pain had I just asked.

I wasted so much time. I made up my own story instead of being direct and asking for the truth. What I learned is that I will never avoid a difficult conversation again. It costs too much. Never be afraid of telling someone you love the truth or hearing the truth from someone you love. Be afraid of the damage that happens when truth is withheld.

Speaking and listening is where healing and growth begins. Sharing our stories is the only way to stand in other people's shoes and make changes that last. This is how we forgive and grow. This is how we heal. This is how we love.

Speak. Heal. Grow. And keep your door open.

Do you need to forgive yourself for something?

_____

_____

_____

_____

CHAPTER 13

The Universe Is Calling. Don't Hang Up.

When you want something, all the universe
conspires in helping you to achieve it.
—PAULO COELHO

One thing we can all count on is that the universe will always tell us the truth. There is nothing I enjoy more than watching the universe call me up and show me the truth. The universe isn't just calling me. It's calling all of us. It's up to us to recognize the call. If we ignore the signs, the signs are left without power to wake us up or move us forward.

The fact that the universe accommodates us exactly when we need it to will never stop amazing me. I feel the energy fields pulling me in the midst of a discovery, in enormous ways, and in very subtle ways. Whether it's the heaviness of rain or the subtlety of sailboats rising back up again, when we pay attention to the signs, we add comfort to our lives, which is why I am always ready to receive messages from the universe.

We all have the power to make things happen. Whether it's a career we want, a partner we want, a house we want, or comfort from a loved one who has passed away, when we visualize what we want, work for what we want, and speak what we want into the universe, the power of that energy multiplies in ways we can't even explain. I've seen this happen in my own life so many times I can no longer call them coincidences.

Remember those terra-cotta urns I used as home base for my childhood games at my grandparent's house? The universe practically delivered them to my doorstep. When we moved from the city to the suburbs, our girls were toddlers, Billy wasn't born yet, and my mom flew to Chicago to help us.

123

When my mom arrived, she said, "Did you know that the people who bought Nana and Pop Pop's house moved to Wilmette?" Wilmette was three towns away from the suburb we had just moved to.

I said, "No, I didn't!"

That's when we pulled out the phone book. For those of you who were born after the launch of the World Wide Web and smartphones, the phone book is a book filled with names, numbers, and addresses. This is how we contacted people in the early 1990s. We quickly found the names of the family who bought my grandparents' house in Gladwyne, Pennsylvania, in the trusty phone book, and without even saying a word, my mom and I grabbed the girls, put them in their car seats, and drove to the address.

When we pulled up to the house, we saw my grandfather's terra-cotta urns. I could not believe my eyes. I started to scream. After Pop Pop died, my nana sold their house, and I remember my mom saying to her, "Mother, don't sell the terra-cotta urns with the house." So my nana sold the terra-cotta urns with the house.

Now the terra-cotta urns and the fabric of my childhood were literally down the street from me. I never left my backyard as a kid, except when I was in my grandfather's yard or in Betsy's yard. It was like my grandfather knew I would break the promise I made to my mom and leave the East Coast and live far away from my family to fulfill my purpose. He sent those terra-cotta urns all the way to Chicago as a way of saying, "Your home base is always here, and your voice is strong."

My mom and I got out of the car, knocked on the door, and introduced ourselves to the owner. She knew who we were immediately, and I thought she was absolutely going to say, "Take the urns!" But she didn't, and for the next twenty-three years, I wrote letters and sent emails offering to purchase the two urns. But still no urns.

Instead I visit the urns all the time. I even park my car, get out, and put my head in the opening of the larger urn and talk to my grandfather. Hearing my voice inside the terra-cotta urn brings back a flood of emotions for me and gives me comfort. I can feel my grandfather's humor and love and hear the power of my voice. Luckily, they sit on the edge of the property, and I haven't been arrested for trespassing yet.

Last year I drove by the house and saw a For Sale sign. My heart sank. "If they move, will they take the terra-cotta urns with them? Will my grandfather leave me? Will I lose the power of my voice? Will I lose my home base?"

So I wrote another letter, and while I don't have the terra-cotta urns yet, I can only pray that the owners will consider my invitation to buy the urns when they sell their home. It has been spoken. It has been written, and therefore, it will happen. Until then, I will continue to visit the terra-cotta urns and feel the connection to my grandfather. I'm sure Joseph Jackson Skelton Jr. has it all worked out for me. And so does the universe.

Ask the universe for what you want. Speak it. Write it. Let it be known. And watch the universe deliver. It may not be exactly what you asked for. Sometimes it's better.

A hard transition from the power of my grandfather's terra-cotta urns to Justin Bieber, but I promise it's worth the awkward turn. In 2009, we took our three kids to the Nickelodeon Kids' Choice Awards in Los Angeles. We have a friend who was a television executive with Nickelodeon at the time, and she kindly hooked us up to the orange-carpet extravaganza.

Marin and Billy had no trouble speaking to the celebrities, who were *all* on the carpet, but Carly could not handle any of it. I had to practically throw her into photos with the stars. Meanwhile, Marin was making eyes with Nick Jonas, and Billy was hanging out with Pete Wentz from Fall Out Boy and Nicole Scherzinger from the Pussycat Dolls. Carly refused to be part of any of it.

When we arrived at the show, Carly pointed to a kid in the audience and said to me, "Mom, that's Justin Bieber."

I'm like, "Who?"

She said, "Mom! He's the boy I'm obsessed with on YouTube."

I said, "Oh, yeah. Right. That kid!"

Justin Bieber was only known to his YouTube following, which at the time was huge, but no one recognized him at The Nickelodeon Kids' Choice Awards. He was a guest of Usher's, Carly's other love, whom she always said she was going to marry, but she had no interest in taking a photo with him.

When we arrived at the VIP after-party, Carly became a new person. She went right up to Justin Bieber, who was standing alone, and said, "Hi! Are you Justin Bieber?" He said yes, almost shocked when she recognized him. Carly was with her cousin Sara, and suddenly, Carly had no inhibitions with Justin Bieber. She asked him for a photo, and when Sara snapped the picture, I can honestly say that I think this was the first fan photo Justin Bieber ever took.

As a person who admittedly adds extra to stories, I obviously can't prove this, but I was there and I am telling you this kid went unnoticed by everyone except Carly Loveman.

Fast-forward the following year, and *Justin Bieber* is now Justin Bieber and is booked on *The Oprah Winfrey Show*—and I happen to be the person in charge of tickets. I asked Carly where the photo was she took with Justin Bieber, and she said she didn't know and asked me why I wanted it. I told her, "I don't know. I just want it." This is known as a mother's intuition, and every child should respect it. But my child, who never wants to be seen, said, "Well, I don't have it."

This was before we took pictures on our phones. We were still snapping photos on cameras, taking the film to photo stores to be developed, waiting a few days to pick them up, and putting them into photo albums. I searched my albums, but there was no photo.

Finally, I asked my daughter Marin if she had the photo, and somehow she found it and gave it to me. Then I gave it to my friend and Harpo photographer, the fabulous George Burns, who has graciously documented so many moments for me, and asked if he could blow the photo up into a five-by-seven for me, which he did.

In the meantime, Carly attended the show along with her cousin Lucy, my sister Cindy's daughter, who flew in for the occasion. Carly and Lucy sat in the studio for Justin Bieber's sound check and later took a photo with Justin Bieber backstage. They were undone.

I was in charge of the meet and greet for the Harpo employee kids who were in the audience. I was told Justin Bieber had a hard out at three in the afternoon, so I kept the meet and greet short and sweet. When it was Carly's turn to take a photo with Justin Bieber, she spoke to him for a few seconds but didn't mention the Nickelodeon Kids' Choice Awards story.

Cue the universe. We finished the photo shoot fast. Justin Bieber left, and I cleared the backstage area in our second studio. Carly and Lucy were exhausted from having spent all morning falling in deeper love with Justin Bieber. I took them to the ladies' room, where Lucy changed out of her Justin Bieber outfit and into her airplane outfit. Then we headed to the Harpo garage, where all good things happen, to get my keys so I could grab Cindy's luggage out of my car and put them in a cab for the airport.

As far as I was concerned, Justin Bieber had left the building because it was long past three o'clock. I opened the side door to the garage, and who was standing alone against the wall looking at his phone? Justin Bieber.

In that moment two options went through my mind. First, I could close the door, turn around, and figure out a way to bypass the garage to get my keys and avoid what I knew would be a complete scene with Justin Bieber. Second, I could keep walking, get my keys, stick with my purpose, pray for the best, and try to keep my job.

I went with the second choice and walked through the garage. Cindy, Carly, and Lucy followed me. I'm not sure who said hello to whom, but suddenly, Carly, Lucy, and Justin Bieber were in a full conversation. My sister Cindy almost collapsed, and my heart was pounding out of my chest.

Carly said, "I met you when you were at the Nickelodeon Kids' Choice Awards, and I think I took your first fan photo with you." Justin Bieber asked Carly if she had the photo.

That's when I glared at Carly and pretty much said with my eyes, "This is why I wanted the photo!" I literally turned around, flew through the door we had just come through, ran up the flight of stairs to my office, grabbed the photo, and returned to the garage in less than thirty seconds. Justin Bieber was still there.

I gave Justin Bieber the photo, and he looked at it and told Carly how different she looked and how much taller he was than her now. As if they were childhood friends, Justin Bieber and Carly Loveman turned around and stood back to back to see how much taller he was than her. I can't make this up.

Justin Bieber autographed the photo and signed his name with a heart on both Carly and Lucy's arms. Then he hopped onto his shuttle bus to leave the magical building where moments like this were normal. The garage door opened, and Carly and Lucy walked out of the garage with Justin Bieber's bus into a throng of screaming girls like they were with Justin Bieber.

Justin Bieber's "U Smile" video came out three months later, and my blonde-haired daughter, who adds extra to her stories too and who wore a side braid in her hair, just like the girl in the video, the first time she met Justin Bieber at the Nickelodeon Kids' Choice Awards, swears the video is based on their encounter. I can't say I disagree because it literally looks like the scene I witnessed. But I am as extra as it gets.

The universe calls us all the time, and we should never hang up and mothers really do know best. When your mother asks you for something, give her that something she has asked you for. I found out later that Carly didn't want anyone to see that photo because she had braces and thought she looked ugly, which is why when Justin Bieber told her she looked different, Carly's entire face lit up.

When Carly asked me why I wanted the photo and I said, "I don't know. I just want it," that should be a reminder that mothers have a sixth sense that should never have to be explained to anyone, especially their child. Do what your mother says, accept her invitations, and live an exciting life!

The crazy part about this story isn't just the "U Smile" video or the fact that Carly found Justin Bieber standing alone twice. It's that seven years after Carly's Justin Bieber moment, the producer of the Justin Bieber show became Carly's boss.

When Carly graduated from college, she was hired as a production assistant for a television talk show executive produced by my friend and mentor Lisa Erspamer, the former executive producer of *The Oprah Winfrey Show.* Lisa brought a team of former *Oprah Winfrey Show* producers and crew to Nashville to make more magic, and Julie, the producer of the Justin Bieber show, became Carly's boss and mentor.

Carly had the opportunity of a lifetime to work with the most talented team in television from *The Oprah Winfrey Show.* She was carrying on my legacy with people I love, and I could not have been more proud. Prior to Nashville, Carly started her television career in the same studio where I started my career with Oprah when she was an intern at *Windy City Live* at WLS-TV. The studio where *The Oprah Winfrey Show* started and where I performed my first audience warm-up is the studio where Carly held her first clipboard.

The universe is so powerful, and I'm always grateful for it. Carly spent a year of her life watching Justin Bieber on YouTube for hours on end. Her love for him created some kind of cosmic pull that no one could possibly explain. I am grateful I didn't lose my job that day in the Harpo garage, and I'm also grateful Carly didn't marry Justin Bieber, even though we are both #Beliebers for life.

Before we moved to the suburbs and discovered my grandfather's terra-cotta urns and before Justin Bieber was born, we lived in a townhouse in Chicago. We loved it, but I always wanted to move to the East Coast and be closer to family.

One day our neighbor, who was a real estate agent, asked us if we were interested in selling our townhouse because she had an interested buyer. For some reason, I said yes. Within a few days, we sold our townhouse, but our plan to move to Philadelphia didn't happen. So we started to look for homes in the suburbs of Chicago, and I hated every house we saw—except one.

We made an offer on the one house I didn't hate, and the sellers accepted our bid. But at the very last minute, I told my husband I didn't want the house. It wasn't because I didn't love it but because I wanted to keep our Philadelphia dream—actually, my Philadelphia dream—alive. So we bailed on our contract, and we rented a fabulous apartment in the city overlooking Lake Michigan. It kind of felt like we were living in New York City, except we weren't.

Two years later when I realized we were never moving to Philadelphia, we looked for a house in the suburbs again, and this time we went through with our contract. It was an adorable cedar-shingle colonial that we rehabbed and made it perfect. Our girls played in our yard, our neighbors welcomed us, and it felt like home. We loved that house and called her the Brown Cow until we painted her gray and we renamed her the Gray Lady.

When Billy was born, we suddenly outgrew the Gray Lady. This is when we made a big mistake. We bought a bigger house that was more than our budget. It was 2001, and mortgages were being handed out like candy on Halloween. So we took the candy and proceeded to lose our investment with each year.

We tried to sell our house in 2008, and you all know how that went. In 2012, after being in our beautiful home for eleven years, it was time for us to get real. We sold our house for a complete loss and needed to find a place to live. The Gray Lady we had sold eleven years prior was suddenly on the market, which I took as a total sign from the universe screaming, "What were you thinking, stupid? You should have never left me!" But we were no longer buyers. We were renters. Going back to the house we should have never left was not an option.

Then the universe called louder. I was sitting at my desk at work, and I saw an email alert of a new listing from our real estate broker in my in-box. The house we had bailed on when we lived in the city eighteen years prior was suddenly available for rent. I started screaming in my office and ran out to where my team sat, and Andy was the only one in the office. I told Andy that I was going to move my family into the house that I should have bought in the first place. Andy was like, "Okay!"

There were very few houses on the rental market in our school district at the time, and the very house we should have bought eighteen years prior was suddenly available for rent. I called my husband, and we immediately called our real estate broker Jody, who, if I actually had my fake reality show *Living Loveman*, would be the first person I would cast because she is the most entertaining human I know. We found out there were at least seven other families trying to rent this house, but what they didn't know was that this house was already mine.

I picked Marin up from her summer internship that afternoon, and her friend Rachel jumped in the car too. Rachel was wearing my dress. (That has absolutely nothing to do with the story, but I add this extra nugget because Rachel was twenty at the time and I was fifty, so I took it as a great compliment that she was wearing my dress.) She had borrowed a dress from Marin's closet that morning for a job interview and had no idea the dress was mine. I told Rachel to keep the dress.

I showed Marin and Rachel the listing sheet and reminded Marin of the story of how we'd almost bought this house when she was two years old. That's when Rachel said, "That's Mike's house."

"What?" I said. Mike was their friend whom I knew well (even though Mike is not his real name). I'm sure Mike would be fine with me using his real name, but in my quest to reduce embarrassment for my children, we'll call him Mike. "Get Mike on the phone now!" I screamed. "Where are the freaking cameras?"

We called Mike and put him on speaker phone, and I asked him to please tell his parents that we would love their home more than anyone could ever possibly love a home. So Mike's parents chose us. And we got to live in the house we should have purchased eighteen years prior. A lot would happen in that house, for better and for worse, but I left that house with a greater understanding of who I really was and what mattered most.

The house taught me what Dorothy learned in *The Wizard of Oz*. I didn't need to go too far to find my heart's desire. I just had to look in my own backyard. This house was always there. I just couldn't see it.

If we aren't growing, we aren't living. I love lessons that smack you right in the face. Every time I drove in the driveway of 1021 Elm Street, our rental house we should have bought eighteen years prior, I said, "I get it now, God."

When it came time for us to buy the home we live in today, my husband suggested we wait a few more years to afford a bigger house. I said, "That's what got us into this mess. I want as little as possible." So we bought a townhouse that fits our life and speaks our truth. I don't need more lessons. Our townhouse address is 18, a number that continues to remind me to live and learn.

On my real last day at Harpo, a place I called home, I was standing in my office alone. Everyone on my team had either left the company or had moved on to other departments. It felt so odd to be the last teammate standing. All of the sudden, a construction crew came into the office and started to take out all the cubicles my team had once sat in. It was like I was watching them disassemble the team I had built. I started to cry.

Their work got louder and dustier, and by the end of the day, what was once my team's office was now being remodeled for someone else's team. As I stood in my office doorway, looking out on the mess, I felt like someone was playing a bad joke on me. And then suddenly, my feelings shifted. My whole body felt the power of the greatest lesson Oprah taught me and taught millions—gratitude.

I was grateful for the years I had worked at Harpo and for all my accomplishments as well as my team's accomplishments. I was grateful for the talented people I was privileged to work with, for the lives we changed, and for the once in a lifetime boss I was called to work for. I was also grateful for the extraordinary people I met, including Holocaust survivor Elie Wiesel.

One day I was simply leaving my office to go to the ladies' room, and there was Elie Wiesel sitting in the reception area. When his eyes met mine, they stopped me in my tracks. I said hello to him, and he stood up. When he held out his hand to shake mine, the power of his story and his handshake gave me goose bumps and shivers from my head to my toes.

I was so honored to shake Elie Wiesel's hand, and when I got to the ladies' room, I sat down on the toilet seat and sobbed my eyes out. Meeting Elie Wiesel was absolutely the most important moment I experienced while inside that magical building. It was truly an honor.

All these thoughts were running through my head like a season finale montage. Producers always see transitions in their lives in video montage form. One scene after another of all the monumental moments flooded my mind. I could almost see Oprah standing in the doorway and telling me it was okay to leave.

And so I left. No fanfare, no confetti, no champagne, no party. Just me quietly leaving a building that gave me more than I could have ever asked for. I thanked the construction crew as I left for giving me the push I needed to walk out the door because I'm not sure I could have made that exit without a push. Sometimes we need a sledgehammer to drive the point home. And so I left the building and thanked the universe for inviting me into the greatest journey of my life.

Cue more magic. I always wanted to work at *TODAY* and have been a longtime fan of the show. I used to visualize myself working there, but I had a three problems.

The first problem was *TODAY* did not have a studio audience and I was an audience producer. The second problem was I lived in Chicago and I still had a child in high school, so I couldn't just leave and go to New York. The third problem was even if I could get a job at *TODAY*, I could never afford to live in New York City, not to mention that my husband could not relocate his job.

When my daughter Marin graduated from college, she landed the NBC Page Program. I was so excited for her, but I have to be honest. I was a little excited for me too. Marin was now my *in* at *TODAY*.

Then Marin got the green room page assignment on *TODAY* and I was like, "Yes, we are getting closer!" Marin ignored me while I continued to drink my morning coffee from my *TODAY* mug and visualized myself working in the offices. The ceilings were low, the lighting was bad, and the offices were crowded with creative and busy TV people.

A year and a half later, I got a call from a former *Oprah Winfrey Show* producer and friend Katy Davis, who asked if I would be interested in consulting for *TODAY* on a new hour they were producing with an audience. It took me less than one second to say yes.

I was on a walk in the forest preserve with Gracie and after I hung up, I remember looking up at the sky thinking that this was crazy! My youngest child was about to leave for college, *TODAY* now had an hour with a studio audience hosted by Megyn Kelly, and my housing was being paid for because I was a consultant.

All three of my problems were resolved just like that. And because my job was temporary, I knew my husband and I would make an adventure out of it and we did. I interviewed for the job, moved to New York City, avoided my empty nest, which I highly recommend, and had the time of my life.

I'm a big fan of the Abraham Hicks daily messages, which are about connection to Source and Source Energy and remind us that we are the creators to our own unique path of joy. The week I arrived at NBC, I received this quote that seemed to sum up my *TODAY* moment for me: "Every time you want something and achieve vibrational harmony with it and allow it to come to you, you not only gain the satisfaction of having accomplished your desire, you also gain a whole new perspective from which to desire."

My whole perspective changed that day, and I realized we can make anything happen we desire.

And guess what? The offices looked just like I pictured them. Low ceilings, low lighting, and crowded with crazy creative TV people whom I fell madly in love with. I got lucky again. Another TV team to call family. Another female boss who empowered me and let me do what I love. I felt like a kid in a candy store. It was so good to be back in another iconic building and part of a new TV team.

The building smelled so good, and just like Harpo Studios, there was a hustle and buzz that made me feel like I was home. I rode the elevators with NBC talent and could barely contain my professional self. I have met countless celebrities, but riding the elevator with Chuck Todd was next level.

Running into Marin and all her work friends had to be a little embarrassing for her. Having your mom show up at your work can't be easy. One day I split my pants at work. I called Marin from my desk and told her she had to go to my apartment and bring me a pair of jeans so I didn't show the *TODAY* team my ass.

I was laughing so hard I could barely breathe. Marin was not laughing at all because at the time she covered the phones for two executives and she couldn't just leave her desk to save her mother's ass. But she did, and thankfully, she kept her job too. Marin did not ask for me to show up at her work, but I did. Carly didn't either, and luckily for her, the universe has kept that from happening twice. I have a feeling it will stay that way.

I have seventeen family members in New York City, eighteen if you include me. My mom is in Philadelphia, and my sister Cindy is in New York City all the time. I started to have what I called "casual family plans," something I had always dreamed of, and my husband commuted to New York.

I saw twelve Broadway shows in six months. I would go to a box office after work and get the cheapest ticket I could find. I'm proud to say I've seen three Evans in *Dear Evan Hansen*, a show I took my family to when it first opened, and it will forever stay on my heart.

I saw Ben Platt, the original Evan in *Dear Evan Hansen*, at Bond 45 having dinner with a friend. I lost my mind. My heart was pounding out of my chest. I was with Carly and Lucy when he walked by our table, and I told them, "This is my Justin Bieber moment!"

When we got up to leave, I walked over to Ben Platt's table, apologized for interrupting him, said hello to his friend, and in thirty seconds, told him how his show impacted my son's life, a seventeen-year-old (at the time we saw the show) musical theater student who suffers from anxiety.

I know he gets the same story over and over again and that it is exhausting for him. He was simply playing a role. But that role impacted our family deeply. It impacted so many families. I told Ben Platt when we were taking our seats at the show that my son Billy told me he didn't want to sit next to me because he knew I would cry the entire time. I went on to say that when he (Ben Platt) hit his first note, Billy was crying right along beside me. Ben Platt smiled and thanked me. He is a kind and talented human. When and if he ever collaborates with Barbra Streisand, call the hospital, because that's where I'll be!

I thanked him for bringing so much talent and heart to a role that will forever stay on our family's hearts and for being nice enough to speak to me while he was having dinner with a friend.

I specifically did not ask Ben Platt for a photo because I do have some boundaries. A year later Ben Platt spoke at the Jewish United Fund's Women's Luncheon in Chicago, and my friend Rachel invited me to sit at her table. Guess who had a meet and greet with Ben Platt? Me! I now have a photo with Ben Platt thanks to some boundaries, my friend Rachel, the JUF, and the good old universe.

My New York City apartment overlooked the Walter Kerr Theater where Bruce Springsteen was on Broadway. The blue lights twinkled in my bedroom every night, calling my name. My dad gave me and my sisters Bruce Springsteen's album *Greetings from Asbury Park, NJ*, when I was ten years old for Christmas. My sisters and I hated Bruce Springsteen's voice, and we thought our dad was crazy.

Soon we would fall in love with Bruce Springsteen's music, and his albums would become the anthem of our childhood, teenage, and college years. I can literally smell the salt of the ocean and feel the cool Jersey Shore breeze when I hear Bruce Springsteen sing.

I entered the ticket lottery for his Broadway show every week and lost every week. Every time I read the email that started with "Unfortunately," I started to like Bruce Springsteen less. This wasn't good. I visited the ticket box office a few times a week and got to know the ushers. But still no tickets.

Here I was, the ticket lady begging for a ticket. When I was walking by the line of ticket holders and saw dads with their ten-year-old sons, I would say to myself, and sometimes out loud, "What do you know about Bruce Springsteen, kid? Give me your ticket!" Thankfully, they didn't hear me, but it made me feel better.

But my attitude was getting dark, and that worried me. So I changed my attitude to a more positive approach, and suddenly, a ticket became available, which was about half the price of the lowest price but still expensive. I saw *Springsteen on Broadway* on a Tuesday night by myself, and to say I loved every second of his show is an understatement. His show was a spiritual, emotional, and religious experience for me, and in my opinion, Bruce Springsteen is the greatest storyteller of our time.

Whether it's Bruce Springsteen, Justin Bieber, Ben Platt, a terra-cotta urn, a dream job at *TODAY*, a house that was always mine, or a sledgehammer that gave me the nudge I needed, I pay attention. The signs are waiting for me, and the signs are waiting for you. It's up to us to see them.

I sometimes think the universe operates like Facebook. Facebook sees what we have previously viewed, bought, or clicked on and leads us to the next thing it thinks we will want to view, buy, or click on. If we use our own data—our professional work experience, our dreams, our desires, the life we want to live, the people we want to live it with, the people who have passed away but to whom we want to stay connected—and we push those thoughts and visions of what we want next and who we want to keep in our lives, those visions become real.

Spend some time with your thoughts. See what your next career looks like, how your audience will embrace you when you speak, where you want to go in your life, and who you want to be beside you. Visualize the things in your life and your career that bring you joy, success, wealth, balance, love, happiness, or any other positive emotion. Then visualize what will bring you that same level of happiness or maybe even more. Invite it in.

LOVESPEAKS LESSON #13: Visualize what you want, speak what you want, recognize what is already yours, and remember that the universe is a powerful source of love. Embrace it.

When people or things you love show up in your life, take them as signs you are on the right path and that everything will be okay. A relationship, a career, and a life don't just happen because you want them. You have to be willing to do the work.

I like to say, "If you see something, *slay* something." When you see something you want, go after it, and do it better than anyone else.

We don't become great speakers just because we see ourselves speaking. We don't live a great life because we want one. We don't get the careers of our dreams because we think they would be cool. Our visual has to be tied to the work we are already doing and the energy we are putting out into the world. We have to be in the trenches. We have to create momentum by doing the work. Momentum moves us forward.

We see what we want because we are so viscerally tied to the work that it is part of who we are. It's in our DNA. As Marion Wright Edelman says, "You can't be what you can't see." Do the work, see what you want, and watch it unfold right before your eyes.

What recently showed up as a sign for you that assured you that it would all be okay?

_____

_____

_____

LOVESPEAKS PRACTICE: Visualize what you want, and produce the story you want in your life. Literally picture it in your mind and see it unfold. Make it real not only by seeing it

---

but also by putting yourself in an environment that will get you closer to what you want. If you want to be a jewelry designer, go to gem shows, and browse jewelry shops. If you want to be a chef, take cooking classes. If you want to be an engineer, then build a robot. Get your mind, body, and soul into whatever it is you want to do.

ALTERNATIVE LOVESPEAKS PRACTICE: Spend some time in prayer, and ask for guidance for what you want. The universe will open itself up to you.

LIVE LOVESPEAKS: Meet Jill. My friend Jill Frank, mother of two and head of Creative Agency Operations at Allstate, starts her story with life coach Marie Forleo's phrase and book title "everything is figure outable." A lover of the words *how* and *why*, Jill says she enjoys the process of figuring things out, which makes her perfect in her role as a producer. She makes things happen and says, "Producing is like a love letter to creation." It's a reminder that we are the producers of our stories and we get to choose what they look like.

My story with Jill is that we both served on an employee council at Harpo, sharing ideas on how to make our great company even greater. I remember in one meeting saying, "I think we should learn how to meditate and then meditate together." We didn't even have time to pee, let alone meditate, so my idea didn't go over so well.

Meditation was not quite as mainstream then as it is now, but I have been practicing energy healing and Reiki since my early twenties, so I am well versed in all things woo-woo. Jill shot me her megawatt smile after I offered my idea and made me feel a little less crazy.

Several years later our extraordinary boss and leader gave her employees the gift of transcendental meditation training, the greatest gift I have ever received, proving not only that *everything is figure outable* but also that the universe is always listening.

When we approach the world with curiosity and allow ourselves to be open to new possibilities, we receive gifts that change our lives. I had absolutely nothing to do with the gift, but I believe the power of my words helped to invite the gift in, and Jill's smile was all I needed to know I was not alone.

I have always been curious. My transformational work didn't start at forty-nine when I was trained in transcendental meditation or at twenty-two when I was diagnosed with psoriasis and psoriatic arthritis and welcomed the practice of holistic medicine or at sixteen when I almost died in a small plane. It actually goes back to when I was four years old. We were passing by a house on Cherry Lane in Wynnewood, Pennsylvania, and from the back seat of my mom's station wagon, I pointed to a house and asked my mom, "Mommy, when did I live there?"

My mom said, "You've never lived there, Sally Lou." But who's not going to believe a four-year-old? I know I have been here before. I also know you have too.

What have you spoken into the universe that showed up in your life?

_____

_____

_____

CHAPTER 14

The Unexpected You

We need to do a better job of putting ourselves
higher on our own "to do" list.
—MICHELLE OBAMA

As a speaker coach, I help people connect with their audience. The unexpected lesson I discovered as a coach is that before we make a connection to our audience, we have to make a connection with ourselves. We have to do the transformational work ourselves before we can connect with others.

Here's another Abraham Hicks quote I happen to love: "You come forth to live happily ever after." While our lives may not be fairy tales, most of us are invested in our happily ever after, and being happy starts with setting time aside for ourselves.

I'm a big fan of the *Oprah & Deepak's 21-Day Meditation Experience.* My former boss always seems to meet me right where I am. It was the summer of 2018, and as I sat in my living room, taking in the message titled "Energy of Attraction—Manifesting Your Best Life," Oprah spoke about our souls. She quoted Gary Zukav from his book *The Seat of the Soul,* who says "When the personality comes to serve the energy of the soul, that is authentic power."

Oprah went on to say, "When we find a way to use our personality to serve what our soul actually came here to do, that is when our connection to ourselves is unstoppable."

I think I hit rewind ten times to relisten to what Oprah said. Her words are packed with so much wisdom. As I sat with her words, I realized it's not only our job to tell our stories; it is also our job to welcome in our personality and allow our personality to serve our soul so we can make a closer connection to ourselves. The personality you have been given is not an accident. It is on purpose.

Talk about a light bulb moment. My personality was given to me on purpose, and it serves what my soul came here to do—to connect with others. It was like fireworks were exploding in my head and my heart. I love it when things make sense. So I ask you, "Are you using your personality to serve what your soul came here to do?"

One thing I know is that you have accomplished your desire to set some time aside for yourself by reading this book, which means you are invested in yourself. When you finish, my hope is that you gain a new connection not only to yourself and the personality you have been blessed with but also to the desire that prompted you to read this book to begin with. My hope is that each day you embrace a life filled with more love, more living, and more speaking.

We are our most important audience, and yet we are the audience that most often gets forgotten. We are the audience we don't make time to connect with. We can all do better. When I find I am disconnected with myself, the first thing I do is meditate. Meditation is my best friend and my home. It's like I hear the click in my head when I'm in meditation that feels like an adjustment in yoga. Mediation is not only good for my heart; it's also good for my head.

Prayer is also a way I stay connected to myself. I can feel disconnection when I have gone a few days without prayer. When I am short on time or exhausted, I say a prayer my minister shared with us one Sunday. It's short and sweet and covers everything. "Thank you, God, for all of it, especially this part of it. Amen." No matter what I am going through, good or bad, I am thanking God for it. You don't have to believe in God to have a daily prayer. You just have to believe in yourself. Pray to you.

Music is another way I connect with myself. I love all music. My all-time favorite song is "September" by Earth, Wind & Fire. My high school friends and I thought the chorus was "Sally Lou Remember" instead of "Say, do you remember," so that's how everyone in my world sings it. September is always the launch of a new television season. It's my January. I will always love and remember September. Whatever your favorite song is, make sure you blast it as often as you can. "Ba dee Yah Sally Lou remember!"

Being the music lover that I am and a believer in doing things out of your comfort zone, I finally made it to Lollapalooza. I went with my friend and music expert Val Haller. I didn't just go one day. I went all four days. I wasn't messing around this time. I was all in. I didn't wear a crop top, I wore Spanx, and I had a ball.

We focus so much on our exterior. What's our weight? Do we need hair color? Do we need Spanx? We focus on work, relationships, parenting, and others, and we should. But we also have to focus on ourselves and what's inside our minds and our spirits. We need to remember to add ourselves to our list and allow ourselves to be playful and daring and also practice mindfulness. Here's a thought: What if we are "the list"? In other words, we don't even have to add ourselves to our to-do list because it's a given that we will always care for ourselves first.

Try something new like dancing or singing karaoke. Share a moment with someone you don't know. Sing out loud, or start a sing-along with strangers or friends. Share a moment with yourself. The goal is to connect to a place that feels a little deeper, more meaningful, and like home—the place that feels like you. That's where all the good stuff lives. That is your home.

The point is to be yourself. It's exhausting trying to be anyone else but you. I never studied anyone when I performed *The Oprah Winfrey Show* warm-up, but as soon as I became a professional speaker, I watched Brené Brown's TED talk and Steve Job's Stanford commencement address, and I fell apart. Who am I to think I am a speaker? And then I realized I can only give my best me, and that's good enough.

You can only give your best you, and that is what makes your presentation and your life brilliant, authentic, powerful, and real. It's what *you* bring to the room that sets you apart from every other speaker and human.

One of my favorite quotes from American mythologist and writer Joseph Campbell is this: "The privilege of a lifetime is being who you are." Oprah introduced this quote to me, and it was painted on a wall on the west side of our Harpo building. Every time I passed it, I was reminded of the privilege of being me. I invite you to allow this to be your new mantra. Repeat it to yourself and you will begin to believe it.

There is so much pressure to be fabulous. What I have learned along the way is that it's okay to be okay. Work on getting the gigs that work for you, not the gigs that work for someone else. You are the only person with your unique talents, your skill set, your likes, and your dislikes.

You are the only person who can decide what smells, sounds, tastes, sights, and feels please you. You are the only person who can say what environment pleases your five senses. You know when you are home, and you know when you are not home. Stick with what feels like home.

I struggle with anxiety. Meditation, prayer, visualization and writing help me manage a disease that is part of my DNA. The Abraham Hicks quote "Worrying is using your imagination to create something you don't want" helps me because it makes sense. When we can make sense of our fears, we can feel our fears begin to ease. My Reiki healer says we need to "ease disease." Whatever brings you ease—whether it's prayer, meditation, mindfulness, music, good nutrition, yoga, exercise, or a nice long walk—keep your body and mind healthy by doing more of it.

I come from a long line of worriers, and sometimes I think my anxiety will never ease. Mom Mom used to answer the phone when I called by saying, "What's wrong?" instead of "Hello!" This is how I am wired. And while I know it will take me a lifetime to conquer the beast of worry, I have found that meditation works better than any pill I have ever taken.

When I was growing up, the only thing I worried about was the bogeyman, and he wasn't even real. Today there are so many real things to worry about we have to take time to quiet our imagination when it takes us down a road of worry and fear. I never thought I would be able to sit still long enough to quiet my mind, and I hear so many people use that excuse. But here's what I know: If I can meditate, so can you.

Once you feel a connection to yourself strengthen, you can feel things begin to fall into place, and you begin to let go of fear. You begin to feel the ease. You discover a new sense of confidence, and you are ready to use your voice as a very powerful tool.

When you are ready to do more speaking, invest in yourself, and practice these tips to prepare yourself for a stage:

- Try out your timing and wit on the people who surround you in your daily life. Think of everyone in your world as your audience.
- Keep a notebook and take notes on what works and what doesn't work, and build your story.
- Spend some time connecting with your most important audience—you.
- Take an improv, storytelling, or stand-up comedy class to strengthen your confidence and delivery.
- Do something brave to open yourself up to more brave things, such as speaking.
- Rehearse! This is where the magic happens. Don't skip rehearsal. In rehearsal, your speech becomes more customized. Like a marathoner adding miles to each run, ideas pop up that are way better than you could have ever written.
- Find a place to rehearse. My car is my favorite rehearsal space. It's small and private, and everything that happens in my car stays in my car. I always bring scripts with me wherever I go, and when I am in between meetings or errands, I practice.
- Block out your speech. I type my entire speech, create a PowerPoint to support it, and make a visual map on one sheet of paper of my entire speech. I'm a visual learner so this is my way of seeing my whole speech at once. Blocking it out helps me see the beginning, middle, and end in one place. It looks like a puzzle of my speech.

When you speak, you will forget something, and it's okay. You are the only person who knows you missed it, so let it go, and keep it moving. Trying to fit in the information you missed is never a good option because it takes you out of the moment. If you can use humor to bring in what you missed, then by all means do it. Humor always works.

Once you own who you are, find a mentor who can help you go after your dream. Nothing makes me happier than when people who have attended my speaker workshop update me on how they are incorporating what they learned into their speeches, workshops, and lives.

We all need people who have our backs. Don't be afraid to ask someone to have yours. It makes you a stronger you. One day you will be a mentor for someone as well if you aren't one already. It's a universal law, and I don't ever break that law. I encourage you not to break that law either because it's never too late to use your talents in an environment that you love. Sometimes we just need a little push from someone else to get us there.

LOVESPEAKS LESSON #14: You are your most important audience. Invest in yourself. Give yourself time to laugh, cry, heal, sing, dance, practice, grow, and share. Make room for mindfulness and stillness every day. Put yourself first on your list. And remember it is such a privilege to be you.

How do you invest in yourself?

_____

_____

_____

LOVESPEAKS PRACTICE: Make yourself a priority every day, and watch how happiness spreads to everyone around you. Speak to yourself in a way you would speak to someone you love. Self-love is essential to engaging with others and with an audience. If you don't take the time to love yourself, you will find others won't take the time either.

Lead by example. Burn a candle, sit by a fire, call a friend, take a walk for the purpose of walking and not exercise, listen to an entire album, clean out your closet, do something totally unexpected that breaks you open and makes you laugh, and write your story.

ALTERNATIVE LOVESPEAKS PRACTICE: Pick the one thing you want to change most in your life and make a plan. Writing an actual plan down not only keeps you honest, it puts the energy out into the world that your plan is real. Leave your plan on Post-it Notes around your house. Set reminders in your phone for a daily update. If you are old school like I am, keep notes in your datebook as a reminder of your plan.

LIVE LOVESPEAKS: We have to have our own backs. If we don't invest in our own time for meditation, self-love, and stillness, we can't offer our best to others. We also have to have a community who has our backs. We have to have *our people.*

Meet Vicki. My friend Vicki Reece is a mother of three and founder of Joy of Mom. Vicki has built a community where she unites millions of moms to help navigate, celebrate, and love motherhood. Vicki starts her story by saying, "Stand up and step up for what you believe in." This tiny package of *wow* packs a mighty message for moms. Her reach through Facebook, Instagram, live streams, and coffee chats is huge—like millions huge.

Vicki is thoughtful, funny, and real and always reminds moms that we are in this together. She says motherhood is universal, but Joy of Mom is different. Vicki says, "We aren't discussing what it means to be a mother. We talk about how it *feels* to be a mother, whether we are exhausted, honored, annoyed, enraptured, uncertain, scared, joyful, full, empty stressed, charged, proud, worried, or a mix on any given day. You have a voice here."

Vicki's unique ability to connect on a deep level allows millions of moms an opportunity to know that someone has their back. It's always nice to know someone has our back. Invest in yourself by finding a community who invests in yours.

Who has your back?

_____

_____

_____

CHAPTER 15

I'm on My Way

Even death is not to be feared by one who has lived wisely.
—BUDDHA

My mentor and the person who has always had my back is my dad, so when my mom called to tell me that he had a stroke, I lost my footing. The world stopped. My mom had just called me the week before to tell me my uncle Scotty had passed away. Now she was calling to tell me more bad news, only this time it was about my dad. I suddenly felt unsteady.

I had already booked a flight to go home for my uncle Scotty's funeral when my mom called, but I was also scheduled to deliver a keynote speech to the Professional Women's Club of Chicago in three days, just two days before my flight. My dad's stroke was not in my plan.

My dad had been struggling with Alzheimer's for several years. He closed his private medical practice when he was eighty-two and stopped teaching medicine at eighty-four. He had given medicine his all. For the first time in my life, I was able to spend so much more time with my dad because he wasn't at the hospital 24-7. Whenever I made a visit to Gladwyne, I never left his side. And he never left mine.

Alzheimer's never stole my dad's personality. The disease slowed him down, but he always had his sweet smile and adorable face. He may have not known if it was breakfast or lunch, but he was always happy no matter what meal he was eating.

When I made him breakfast and gave him a cup of coffee, his whole face lit up. He started to remind me of his brother Jody. I called my dad "Snack Man" because he would open up the refrigerator and stand in front of it, deciding what snack he was going to make himself in between meals. He had the diet of a teenage boy and somehow managed to stay in teenage boy shape.

When he was diagnosed with Alzheimer's, the doctors asked him questions. "What's your zip code? What was your grandmother's name?" My mom laughed because he didn't know the answers to these questions before he had Alzheimer's, so he certainly wasn't going to know them with Alzheimer's.

But my dad could tell the story about the time he hit the goalpost and lost the soccer game at Rutgers University without one detail missing. He could also sing every word to his alma mater song and every college fight song ever written. And his Cynwyd Clown stories were always intact.

I would sit with my dad for hours and listen to his stories. My son Billy, his namesake, would do the same. We all did. We hung on his every word. Billy is my father's first boy. My two sisters each have three girls, and I have two girls. Billy was born into a family of girls, and when my dad first held him, I caught him looking in the mirror and saying, "Look, two Billies!"

When Billy got the lead role in the eighth-grade musical, my entire family traveled to Chicago for his first performance in *Little Shop of Horrors*. I said to my dad, "The one boy you have is in musical theater and not a soccer player. Are you going to be okay?" My dad smiled and couldn't have been prouder of his musical theater grandson. He also couldn't stop singing "Suddenly Seymour" for the next few months.

I always wanted to make a documentary titled *Running with Billy* because my dad never stopped moving, but I never did because I was too busy with my own work. Instead I sat down with my dad toward the end of his life and videotaped his stories in a lucid moment during one of his last visits to Chicago. I treasure that recording and call it *Sitting with Billy*.

My mom told me that my dad's stroke was mild. But he couldn't walk or talk. My brother-in-law Jud, whom I've known since I was eleven years old and who is the older brother I always wanted, carried my dad upstairs to my parents' bedroom, and the next thing I was told was that Uncle Scotty's hospice bed was being delivered to our house and his hospice nurse was on her way. The Cynwyd Clowns were taking care of their own.

It still didn't dawn on me that things were getting bad. I had just seen my dad two months before his stroke when I flew home for my uncle Tom's funeral. (Uncle Tom was my mom's sister's husband.) My dad had dressed himself in a handsome suit and just before we left for the funeral service, I videotaped him, which I was doing more of as he began to age.

He said, "I'm dressed to go to a funeral, which doesn't make me very happy. But I think that this suit and the pants and the whole thing looks pretty doggone good on me. And I will try to be a happy guy in the face of what is terrible. But I have the suit. I have the tie. I have everything on the way I have it. And that will get me through." He was very proud that he had dressed himself properly. He was very sad and totally cute.

A few weeks after the funeral, my dad slipped on his bathroom rug in the middle of the night and was hospitalized with a brain bleed. I flew home, and miraculously, he managed to heal without needing brain surgery. Maybe it was this fall, his previous falls, and probably a lot of soccer headers that caused my dad to have a stroke.

A week before my dad's stroke, he said to my mom, "Snookie, I need to go. Tommy is calling me." My mom had no idea what my dad was talking about at first, but then she realized he was talking about Uncle Tom. My dad was being called, and we were on alert.

I needed my dad to be stable for the next three days. I am not sure how it all happened. I'm assuming it was a combination of the universe, magic, God, and my dad, but I managed to get lost in my work, and my dad waited for me. He waited for all of us. Unbeknownst to me, while I was speaking, my husband booked a flight home for me because my family had called him. My dad was *on his way*, I didn't have another day to wait and I needed to get home.

When I arrived at my parents' house, with my daughter Marin who traveled with me, it was two in the morning. My sisters were already there. I walked into my parents' bedroom and saw my dad and fell apart. I was not prepared. Any prior loss I have had, I was on my way to say goodbye and missed my opportunity. I always thought God was protecting me from seeing the people I loved die. I didn't think I could handle it, and it turns out I couldn't. As soon as I saw him, I hid under my dad's hospice bed like I used to hide in the closet when Jody choked, as if hiding would make it all go away.

When I got out from under his bed, I begged my sisters to please take our dad off hospice and do everything we could to save him. That's when they sat me down and showed me his living will. I began to come to terms with how my dad wanted to leave this world. He was a doctor. He had spent his whole life saving other people's lives. He didn't want his life to be saved if he couldn't save others.

Before my dad's stroke, we were beginning to talk about next steps. Would we have to put him in a home? Would we bring in full-time care? Neither plan was a good one. We don't do homes in our family, and we don't want help. This is the Oaks way. We are mighty, and we are strong. We take care of our own. And so I said, "Okay."

My sisters started to administer morphine. I couldn't handle that, and they could. But not easily. It was absolutely awful, and I will forever be in gratitude for their strength. There were a few moments where it looked like it was time and my dad was on his way, but Carly, Billy, and my husband had not arrived from Chicago yet. They were driving because Carly had just had her tonsils out and couldn't fly.

We were racing against the clock. I started to play music my dad loved. Our song was "Raindrops Keep Falling on My Head" from the film *Butch Cassidy and the Sundance Kid*. We used to turn it up really loud in his 442 Cutlass convertible and drive around like we were a couple of outlaws. I found the song on a Pandora station of '70s music, and it made him happy.

Then the Carpenters song "Close to You" came on. We played it over and over again, and every time the song played, my dad's eyes would light up. "Close to You" became our anthem. "On the day that you were born, the angels got together and decided to create a dream come true." I truly believe angels brought my dad to this earth and angels were going to take him home.

Carly, Billy, and my husband made it in time. We all made it in time. No one was missing—twenty of us circling my dad's bed, holding his hands, stroking his head, singing him songs, and telling him how much we loved him.

I remember looking around the room and saying, "I want to write about this one day." So I did. My dad could not have written a more perfect script to the ending of his life. To steal one of his favorite words, it was *phantasmagorical*! We were all there. There was no unfinished business. We stood as a strong circle of love, sending him back to the angels. I specifically said to my dad, "This is not over, Dad. I expect you to be in touch with me daily." I put my cross in his hand and told him he was the greatest father to have ever lived.

When we weren't singing his favorite songs from the '70s, we were singing Christmas carols. It was June, and we are not normal. My dad's face lit up when his great-grandchildren August, my dad's second boy, and Margot entered the room. It was as if the heavens had parted and the angels were singing. There was his adorable face again, loving the next generation of Team Oaksie.

When Jud entered the room, my dad's face filled with urgency. I knew what he was thinking. Jud was the only man with whom my dad could possibly ensure his family's safety and well-being. I told him, "Dad, don't worry. We know Jud's got us." And he calmed down. There hasn't been a time since that when I've seen Jud and he hasn't said, "I've got you."

It was now Friday, the day I was supposed to have traveled home for my uncle Scotty's funeral. It was late in the evening, and the kids and our husbands said their goodbyes to my dad and went back to the hotel to sleep. It was rough. None of us were certain what the night would bring, but I don't think any of us thought our dad would die that night.

My mom, my sisters, and I stayed with my dad and his hospice nurse. We were exhausted. I called my friend and Harpo teammate Sharvo. (Her real name is Sharvonne, but no one calls her that.) Sharvo had recently lost her mom and dad, and we share what we call "witchery." Good witches of course! Let's just say we are both very tuned in. I told her that my dad looked like he was ready to go but something was holding him back. Sharvo asked me, "Has everyone given him permission?"

I said yes.

My sisters needed sleep. They were taking turns administering the morphine, and it was exhausting, emotionally and physically. They went to sleep, and my mom did too. I was sleeping on my parents' bedroom floor. The hospice nurse told me to go lie down in the other room. I told her I didn't want to leave my dad, but she pretty much forced me to go. I made her pinky-promise that she would wake me up if there were any changes. We pinky-promised.

I guess this was the permission my dad needed. He needed us to leave him alone. My sisters woke me up when they came upstairs a few hours later to give my dad his morphine dose. It was just after three in the morning. I'm not even sure what they said to me, but I realized my dad was gone. His hospice nurse must have fallen asleep, and my dad quietly took his last breath without any of us in the room to witness his passing. He was never a fan of goodbyes.

My dad was on his way, and I was devastated. My first call was to Sharvo, who assured me that this was why my dad wasn't ready to go yet. We wouldn't leave him alone, and he didn't want to take his last breath in front of us. He was a doctor. He had seen people take their last breath, and he wanted to spare us from seeing him do the same. Four years later it makes sense to me. But it will take a long time for me to forgive myself. I'm working on it.

Suddenly, it was over. Now what? My mom got into bed with my dad and laid with him until the funeral home director arrived. I could not handle this part. In fact, I don't even know where I went and have no memory of what happened next.

The sun was coming up, and our kids and husbands were arriving from the nearby hotel. We were all comforting one another. It was the most devastating feeling, and yet there was peace and a little relief our father, grandfather, father-in-law, great-grandfather, and husband was no longer in pain. Suddenly, we realized it was Uncle Scotty's funeral, and we were now able to attend.

I know this sounds crazy, but it was the truth. I don't know where we found the strength, but clearly, it was from my dad. Somehow we managed to get dressed and paid our respects eight hours after losing our dad to his best friend and fellow Cynwyd Clown. We upheld the Cynwyd Clowns' slogan "First in peace. First in war. Cynwyd Clowns forevermore."

When Uncle Scotty's son Rip saw me after his father's service, he said, "Hey, Lulu, how's Oaksie?" Oaksie was my dad's nickname. I looked at him and said, "He passed away this morning." Rip looked at me like I had lost my mind. And I had. We all had.

Marin and I stayed the week with my mom, and so did my sister Cindy. Everyone else went home the next day and returned for the funeral the following weekend. Cindy and I were now in charge of the funeral, and we had not recovered our minds. I went into full producer mode, and Cindy went into executive producer mode. We were unstoppable.

I was counting the seats in the church like I counted the seats in *The Oprah Winfrey Show* studio. There weren't enough. Even adding folding chairs wouldn't get us the number we needed, and we were about to violate every fire marshal code. We asked if we could use the choir stalls for seating, and the church said yes. But we still needed more seats. Then we asked if we could put up a tent for extra seating outside, and the church said yes.

We googled audiovisual companies and hired the first person who took our call. We didn't even get a referral or do a Yelp search. We were moving fast and taking chances. A man picked up our call and said, "This is Bill," and we said, "Bill! We like your name. You're hired!" We were leading with our hearts, which is how we operate.

The tent went up. The video screens and cables were installed so we could feed the video of the service from the church into the tent. We wiped down the seats from the morning dew, something I've done one too many times on remote shows. Marin made photo collages and a video of my dad, and we ordered maroon and white leopard paw fans to go on every seat in honor of my father's love for Lafayette College, home of the leopards.

My niece Kristen, who has her PhD in English literature and is a gifted writer, wrote my father's obituary. It was a work of art. We ordered boxes of Tic Tacs, a candy my dad always had in his pocket, to give to everyone as they left his service. And my mom just kept wondering what the hell we were doing.

I was carrying around my clipboard at the church, and I noticed that the strangest-looking bugs were hanging out on it. They were not houseflies. They were cute little bees that would not budge even when I tried to shoo them away. *OMG, it's happening!* I thought. *My dad is already keeping in touch.* Bee was staying close to me. The cute little bees would continue for another year, and I knew when the visitations were my dad and when they were not. It's a physical feeling that I can only explain as *knowing*.

The funeral was magnificent. Seven hundred people attended. Jud spoke. Cindy spoke. Susan spoke. I spoke. And my niece Kelly spoke. Kelly actually was my dad's favorite, and we are all okay with that. We laughed, we cried, we celebrated. There was applause. Lots and lots of applause. We told our funeral director that we put the *fun* in funeral, and we did. We sang "Joy to the World" and "Close to You," which may have been a funeral first.

A man came up to me before the service started and said, "I was the last patient your dad saw before he retired. I'm so grateful." What a gift it was for me to meet this man. The choir stalls were filled with young men who were current Lafayette College soccer players and alumni who played soccer. It was the most magnificent visual we could have ever planned for seeing the stalls packed with athletes my dad mentored.

That morning three of my college friends who played soccer at Lafayette—Benji, Woody, and George—texted me a photo of their morning run dedicated to my dad. They were wearing Lafayette soccer jerseys. They didn't attend the funeral for me. They attended the funeral for my dad. They each had their own friendship with my dad, and I loved that.

After the service incoming freshman soccer players introduced themselves to me. I didn't understand why they were at the funeral since they had never met my dad. One of the players told me he couldn't be a part of the program without knowing Dr. Oaks and that was why he was there. For their fall season, the Lafayette men's soccer team wore a patch on their jerseys that said "The 12th man" for my dad.

My dad made his mark. His legacy lives on in all of us as well as in the soccer players and athletes he mentored, the medical students he taught, and the patients he cared for. These stories continued throughout the day, the week, the month, and the year. People still tell us how our dad changed their lives. What a gift to have a father who meant so much to so many.

Speaking about the people we have lost ensures their lives never end. Writing about them brings the same blessing. This book has brought my dad, my grandparents, and my uncle Jody closer to me, and the comfort I feel when I write about them is a gift I wish for everyone to experience.

Even if three people read this book, my mom and my two sisters, I will have accomplished the very thing I set out to do, namely to connect with others through my story and also to connect with myself. The unexpected gift is that writing this book has connected me to the people I have lost. It's like they are standing right beside me, which has actually made it difficult for me to finish this book. I never want that feeling to end.

LOVESPEAKS LESSON #15: Keep the people you love *close to you* and celebrate them in life. Don't wait for a reason to celebrate. Find a reason to celebrate them right now. This is not a dress rehearsal. This is life. Life is for the living. Tell your people you love them. Let your love speak.

If you have lost people you love, write about them and feel the gift of their presence in your life. The simple act of writing brings those we have lost closer to us.

Who do you need to say I love you to?

_____

_____

_____

LOVESPEAKS PRACTICE: If there is someone you love who you haven't seen in more than a year, make a plan to see the person. Don't let time separate you from people you love. We all get busy. And the next thing you know, a decade goes by, and you've missed out on a relationship that you once cherished.

The only way to stay close to the people we love is to spend time with them. Time is not always on our side. Make use of time while you have time.

ALTERNATIVE LOVESPEAKS PRACTICE: If travel is an expense and not in your budget and that is the reason why you have not seen someone you love, make a date to call, Skype, or FaceTime your friend or family member. Remember that text threads keep families and friends close too. We have so much technology at our fingertips to keep us connected. Use it.

LIVE LOVESPEAKS: For all the reasons why social media is bad, there are so many reasons why it is good. We live all over the world and are separated from family and friends. Social media connects us and keeps us close. Use it to connect to your world. I am in touch with so many high school friends through Instagram and

Facebook. I have not seen many of them in almost forty years, but if I saw them tomorrow, we would not skip a beat.

My Harpo family lives all over the country, but we stay in touch in our private Facebook group. We not only make one another laugh, but we also offer resources and opportunities to one another just like we did when we worked together.

My family, whom I see the most in my life but who all live on the East Coast, is the main reason I love social media. We laugh hysterically when we send one another a silly Snapchat with a filter (I can't be left alone with a phone and Snapchat filters) or tag one another in posts we know will make us laugh.

I read stories about other people's families and feel the love others share. This is the upside of social media. Love it for that reason alone, and connect with people who matter to you. It's the next best thing to being there. But there's nothing like being there, so do both if you can.

Call the person whose name you wrote in this section, and make a date to let this individual know how much you love him or her.

What is it about the person whose name you wrote in this section you are most grateful for?

_____

_____

_____

CHAPTER 16

Love Never Leaves

Finding gratitude and appreciation is key to resilience.
—SHERYL SANDBERG

My dad died on June 13 just after three in the morning. Maybe it was even three thirteen, but we will never know. All I know is that the numbers three and thirteen keep appearing since my dad passed. My daughter Marin moved to Thirteenth and Third Avenue in New York City a month after my dad died. I wake up at three thirteen all the time, and when I look at the clock, I just smile.

Recently, I woke up at four forty-two in the morning. My dad's favorite convertible, the one we rode around in like a couple of outlaws, was his Oldsmobile Cutlass 442 he called the "Orange Tomato." My dad was changing up his numbers, and I was impressed.

When I dream about my dad, I feel they are visitations. I still have his cell phone number saved in my phone, and just when I need him, my phone dials it on its own. Okay, I never lock my phone, but the fact that my phone chooses to call my dad's number and not one of the other hundreds of contacts I have is proof my dad is by my side.

I find letters he has written to me over the years just when I need them most and notes he has written as well. My dad wrote us letters after big life events like graduations. And after every visit with us, my dad would leave us a note. They weren't long. They were just his way of leaving a piece of himself. His notes were part of his superstitious rituals. We all struggle with separation, and this was my dad's way of reminding us he is always with us, which was way better than saying goodbye.

I am so grateful for every letter or note my dad took the time to write to me and to my family. My favorite note captures my dad in every way. It hangs on my kitchen wall, and it simply says, "To my wonderful team! Marin, Carly, Billy. Love you all so much. God bless. Papa."

Nine months after my dad passed away, my mom welcomed her thirteenth girl. Sylvia June, my mom's great-granddaughter, who was born on March 26. Twenty-six is my mom's favorite number because June 26 is her birthday as well as my parents' wedding anniversary, and thirteen times two equals twenty-six. My mom's childhood address was 313 Landrillo Road. The power of these numbers began long before my parents ever met and continues to remind us love never leaves.

I hear "Close to You" all the time. We were in London visiting Andrea and Pete during Christmas (one of two I missed in Gladwyne), and there was live music at the restaurant where we were having dinner. I excused myself to go to the ladies' room, and as I was washing my hands, I could hear the band playing "Close to You." I ran for the bathroom exit and crashed into my kids, who were running in to get me. There he goes again, keeping his promise. For a guy who never really left Philadelphia, I was happy he made it to London!

When it was time for Carly to go back to Lafayette College for her junior year the fall after losing my dad, I knew it would be hard for her to be on campus without him. It's not a normal thing for a college kid to think about, but I think it's obvious by now we are not a normal family. My parents were on that campus all the time, and most grandparents don't drop off their granddaughters at fraternity parties. Mine do.

We made a visit to Cindy's beach house at the Jersey Shore before I took Carly back to school. As we were leaving, my mom gave me a box of some of my father's ashes. I said, "Why are you giving these to me?"

My mom said, "I don't know. I just want you to have them." Her words sounded familiar, so I took the ashes because I never question my mother's sixth sense.

I tucked the box away in my carry-on bag, and I felt very strange carrying my dad around with me in a box. We got up to school, and I moved Carly into her room at her sorority house. This is usually my husband's job, but I offered to do the college move this time because I wanted to be at Lafayette and close to my dad.

The next day I said goodbye to Carly. It was emotional, and we were both struggling. As I crossed the campus—my campus and the campus my father, daughter, sisters, nieces, and brother-in-law attended—to go back to the hotel where a car was waiting for me to take me to the Philadelphia airport, I got a text from my niece mentioning that it was the season opener for the men's soccer team at Oaks Stadium. How did I not know this? I was so upset and wished I had known so I could have represented my dad and gone to the game and taken a later flight.

And then it hit me. My father was with me. He had never missed a Lafayette College men's soccer season opener, and he wasn't about to miss this one! I asked the driver if he could take me out to Oaks Stadium before we went to the airport. He said yes, and off we went to the field.

I have felt excitement in my life so many times—Christmas Eve excitement, Christmas morning excitement, the excitement of giving birth, the excitement of waiting for my family or children to arrive in my driveway for a visit, the excitement of surprising my family with a visit, and all the exciting moments I had at *The Oprah Winfrey Show*—but this excitement was something I can't even begin to explain. It was filled with purpose, and it was the most healing kind of excitement I have ever experienced.

When I arrived at Oaks Stadium, I ran out of the car and onto the field where the opposing team was already practicing, and the Lafayette team had not come out yet. I was out of breath and found an assistant coach and asked him where Dennis, the head coach, was.

I saw Dennis coming onto the field, and I told him, "My dad is here for your season opener!" I showed Dennis, who was one of my father's pallbearers at his funeral, the box. He looked up at the sky and kissed the box, and then I sprinkled some of my dad's ashes under the team's bench and on the thirteenth step where my dad stood for every game.

I got back into the car with the rest of my dad's ashes and rode to the airport with my dad and an extremely full heart. I was certain my dad was standing on that field, watching the season opener, and I'm also certain he's been at every home game since.

On September 7, eighty-seven days after my father passed away and the age my father was when he passed away, I had a dream about my dad. We were all together at a football game, and he started to fall. I caught him, and my dad died in my arms. When I woke up, I was crying. I was still struggling with not having been with my dad when he died. I kept my eyes shut for a moment, and when I opened them, I looked at the clock. It was five twenty-three in the morning. But what did that mean?

I woke my husband up to tell him about my dream, and he started to cry. I had an overwhelming feeling to hear my dad's voice. It was like I had to hear it. My husband got up to use the bathroom, and I got out of bed to look for the scrapbook my husband had made for me when *The Oprah Winfrey Show* ended. My dad had written me a beautiful letter about watching me perform the warm-up at the United Center, and my husband included it in the scrapbook. I wanted to read the letter so I could hear my dad's voice.

I brought the scrapbook back to bed and opened it up to read the letter. I felt so much love hearing my dad's words in my mind and in my heart, and my entire body felt comforted. He wrote, "Just another magic moment for the Oaksie team. We are all so very proud, and I will love you forever."

Then I looked at the date of the letter—May 23, 2011. That's 5/23 ... or 5:23. I began to howl like a wild animal. My husband came running back into the room, and I showed him the date and explained the time on the clock. This was another visit from my dad, and it was a big one.

Two months later, Marcy offered me two tickets to see a medium named Thomas John do a reading at the Wilmette Theater. I declined her invitation because while I love mediums, I don't love psychics, and Thomas John is also a psychic. But as you know, I also don't like saying no to invitations from anyone who loves or likes me, so I finally said yes. My husband and I went to see Thomas John.

There were a little more than a hundred people in the theater, and Thomas John's first question was if October 12 or 18 meant anything to anyone. Even though October 12 is my father's birthday and eighteen is one of my favorite numbers, I was not about to raise my hand right out of the box. Thomas John moved on, and he read other people from new information he was giving.

Then he said, "Has anyone recently lost a father figure in Pennsylvania who was in the medical field?" Clearly, my dad was not giving up. I raised my hand. My heart started to pound. I looked at my husband and said, "It's happening." Thomas John called on me, and I said, "Yes, my father."

Thomas John said, "This may sound really strange, but your father has the most adorable face." Okay, you can't google that! Now a microphone was in my face, and for the first time, besides being in the cafeteria with Miss Baker, I was terrified to speak.

Thomas John continued with stories you can't google. "Your mom and dad went to a lot of football games together?"

"Yes," I said.

"I see them in the bleachers a lot. He's in the bleachers. Your mom doesn't always want to go to the games now, but she goes to be close to your dad."

I had just dropped my mother off that morning at O'Hare to go home to Philadelphia. I wanted her to stay and go to the reading with me, but she had no interest. I asked her what she was doing over the weekend, and she said, "I guess I'm going to go up to Lafayette for the football game. I don't want to go, but I want to be close to Dad." Seriously, was Thomas John in the car with us?

Then Thomas John asked me, "Are you writing a book?"

"Yes," I said. (I was writing this one actually.)

"Your dad wants you to write it. Keep writing," he said. My dad was always writing a speech or a book. I am my father's daughter. I look like him. I think like him. I worry like him. I love like him, and I act like him. My dining room table, where most of this book was written, was starting to look like my sister's beach house table where my dad spent much of his retirement writing.

He set up his papers, all handwritten, and he would write all day. There was no sense of order because his Alzheimer's wouldn't allow him to stay focused, but writing brought him great pleasure and healing, and it has done the same for me. My dad has been published in medical journals, but he never published the book he was trying to write at Cindy's beach house, so I write mine for my father.

Thomas John went on to say, "He's with a younger sibling who passed." That was Jody or my aunt Sally Lou. "He misses your mom. He misses dancing with her," he continued. My parents danced beautifully together, and I have so many videos that capture their love. "Is there a scholarship

161

in his name?" Thomas John asked. "Yes, Oaks Leadership Academy." He finished, "He will continue to come to you in your dreams. He is a force that is bigger than most spirits."

I felt my father's presence from the top of my head to the bottom of my toes. As far as I was concerned, my dad was in the room. And for the skeptics, even if he wasn't, he was for me. And that's all that matters.

I decided to have a small service for my dad in Chicago because I wanted a place to go to feel his presence that was close to me. Maple Street Park in Winnetka is where we have our summer church services, and it overlooks the lake, my place of healing. We sat with our rabbi Steve and our minister Christopher individually and talked about my dad after we lost him.

I shared with Christopher that my dad received a Thousand Points of Light Award from President George Hoover Bush for his work at the St. John's Homeless Clinic in Philadelphia. I explained that he also started a soccer team for the men who lived at the shelter. This was my dad's dream—to give these men the feeling of a team where they could work together for a common goal. He also knew that if the men got in shape, they would feel better about themselves.

There was a man at the shelter who wouldn't come up from the basement or play on the team. When my dad held clinic hours at the shelter, he went down to the basement to examine this man. It was the only time this man had any human contact. My dad was his only connection to the world.

In honor of my father's sixtieth anniversary of graduating from Lafayette College and four years before his death, my sister Cindy and my brother-in-law Jud started Oaks Leadership Academy, which supports Lafayette student-athletes and coaches in their quest to become effective leaders in academics, athletics, and life.

Close to three hundred students have been trained through the academy to date. This is also my father's legacy and a beautiful gift from Cindy and Jud. This is how my dad lived his life. He developed young people into leaders who make the world a better place. Now there will be young leaders who will never meet my dad, but they will learn so many of his lessons.

After his death the men's soccer players and the soccer alumni community along with Cindy and Jud commissioned a statue that sits on the spot where my father watched every game next to the thirteenth step at the stadium. It's a bronze soccer ball with my father's name engraved on it as well as the year of his graduating class. Before the team takes the field for every home game, they touch the top of the ball for good luck in the same way that they used to high-five my dad when he stood there. This is another part of the Billy Oaks legacy.

I am so grateful I made the choice to attend Lafayette College and not a big university to study television. Whenever I am on campus, I feel my dad's spirit. I see his adorable face, and I hear his voice. Students, faculty, athletes, and alumni come up to me and say, "You're Dr. Oaks' daughter?"

"Yes, I am." And I'm right back in the hospital hallways feeling proud to be connected to someone so loved.

LOVESPEAKS LESSON #16: We may lose people we love, but they never leave our lives. That's the unexpected gift. While every loss is gut-wrenching, if we practice keeping those we have lost alive, the comfort becomes real. It's moments of peace that we all want. Every moment I have had with my dad since he has passed has given me a sense of resilience I never could have imagined.

How do you stay connected with a loved one you have lost?

_____

_____

_____

LOVESPEAKS PRACTICE: Prayer and meditation have fine-tuned my access to those I have lost, and it will help to fine-tune yours if you are looking for access. If you are struggling with a loss, I encourage you to meditate and spend some time in prayer, and you will feel some relief and connection. You will open up your vessel to a world that can bring you great comfort.

ALTERNATIVE LOVESPEAKS PRACTICE: Spend some time looking at photographs or videos of people you have lost. Use the power of your thoughts to help call them into your life. Consult a professional or find a support group if you are struggling. Connection is always a beautiful way to healing, but sometimes we need professional help.

LIVE LOVESPEAKS: I never thought I would be able to handle losing my dad. It hasn't been easy. No loss is. But the new relationship I have with him on a spiritual level and the lives that continue to be changed by my father are the unexpected gifts that have made living life without him a little bit easier.

I woke up recently when I heard the words *we have*. I am not sure who spoke them, but I know I didn't, and neither did my husband. My body felt illuminated when I heard the words. I looked at the clock, and it was three thirteen in the morning. *Hi, Dad.*

But what does *we have* mean? I wondered. I spent some time in quiet meditation, and the next morning my own words came to me, "It's better to have than not to have had at all." Appreciate the moment, every person, and every breath. Appreciate what *we have* while *we have* it.

I do not take lightly that I was raised well in a loving and supportive family. It is a privilege. I see the pain and suffering people have from being raised in homes that were not supportive and loving like mine. My life has been made easier because of my parents and I am grateful every single day of my life that God blessed me with them. I am privileged to be an Oaks. I pray for others who do not have this fortune. And I try to spread love in my small way to help others feel a piece of what I was blessed to have grown up with.

I could not have found faith and forgiveness had it not been for the unconditional love my parents gave me and my sisters. I have passed these lessons along to my children. Yes, my children have scars. But their scars don't just represent pain. They represent resilience, empathy, forgiveness, and truth. Along with my husband, my children are the three people I enjoy spending time with the most, so I hope we have done something right.

Who do you appreciate the most in your life, and why?

_____

_____

_____

CHAPTER 17

Accept Invitations from Your Daughter

Wherever you are, that is your platform, your stage, your circle of influence. That is your talk show, and that is where your power lies.
—OPRAH WINFREY

I was able to fulfill my career dream that started with an invitation from my mother and a clipboard. I hope at some point someone saw me from their audience seat and said, "I want to do *that!*" Maybe I have inspired someone the same way the girl with the clipboard inspired me. Maybe you have too.

I had the great honor of inviting my mom to the *Watching Oprah* exhibit at the Smithsonian Museum of African American History and Culture, and after she said no a few times to my invitation, she finally said yes. Our tickets were for the Sunday after Thanksgiving, and my family and I were driving to Washington, DC, from Cleveland, where we celebrate the holiday with my husband's family.

My mother was traveling from Philadelphia, and my plan was to pick her up at Union Train Station when she arrived in Washington, DC. But she was nervous to travel home alone on Sunday because she was scared the train would be too crowded with holiday travelers. So she kept saying no to my invitation.

My husband's plan was to drive back to Chicago while the kids and I returned to our respective cities via plane or train. He offered to drive my mom home to Gladwyne on his way back to Chicago so she wouldn't have to take the train. Gladwyne is not exactly on the way home to Chicago, but my husband knew how important this invitation was to me. He also knew my mom was way too smart to think this was normal.

So we tricked my mom into accepting the ride. We told her we had to pick up my toboggan at her house so we could get it back to Chicago. My mom had been complaining about my childhood toboggan being in her garage for a few years. In seventh grade I left my toboggan at my friend Jimmy Liacouras's house. A few years ago, I saw Jimmy at the local gas station in Gladwyne. Jimmy lives in Greece, but he happened to be in town, and we both happened to be getting gas at the same time.

Immediately when I saw him, I said, "Hey, Jimmy! Where's my toboggan?" It was as if no time had passed. He said, "It's at my parents' house. They're moving, and I'll drop it off to your mom's house." And just like that, I got my toboggan back forty-one years later.

What I didn't know is that my toboggan would come in handy as an excuse for my mother to accept my invitation to the *Watching Oprah* exhibit a few years later. I wanted to repay my mom for her invitation to *The Mike Douglas Show* with an invitation of my own. I wouldn't stop until she said yes because my invitation was important to me.

Before I even got into the exhibit, I stood in front of the donor wall at the entrance of the museum in front of Oprah Winfrey's name. Tears started streaming down my face. She is the lead donor of the museum, and what a story she has to tell. There is no story that could possibly compare to hers. The power of it is unimaginable. It is an act of God. It is pure magic.

I had the great privilege of calling her my boss, and suddenly, I got very emotional. I was loving her story like it was my job because it is. It was. And it always will be. It's so beautiful to love someone else's story as well as our own. That's when we really feel our connection to humankind.

Once we entered the exhibit I had what I would call an out of body experience. I felt like I was floating through time. The wall of the 4561 show titles we produced was staggering. I knew every person featured in the exhibit by name, and they knew mine. Every voice I heard on the videos was the voice of a friend.

Oprah's story was well known to me, but seeing it in a museum just made me wonder how I got to be so lucky to have moved to a city the same year she did with a dream to work on a talk show. That doesn't just happen. There is a force behind it that can only be called the universe and God. Oprah Winfrey changed the world, and continues to change the world. And I was so lucky to be her student.

As my mom and I stood in front of the wall that displayed my name and a quote I gave about how we booked the studio audience in the old days, I felt the power of my mom accepting my invitation.

My quote said, "The trick was getting the right audience for a given topic. Back in the day we'd put voice-overs at the end of soap operas: 'If you are cheating on your husband, call this number.' Then we'd spend all afternoon answering the phones: '*Oprah Show*, please hold *Oprah Show*, please hold. *Oprah Show*, please hold.'"

Not exactly the quote I would have picked to best represent my contribution to *The Oprah Winfrey Show*, but I'm in the freaking Smithsonian, so I'm not going to complain! Honestly, I was speechless.

My quote gave me an opportunity to say to my mom, "Look, Mom. I'm in the Smithsonian!" That doesn't just happen every day. I thanked my mom for accepting my invitation, and I thanked her for giving me a beautiful start to my story. I also thanked her for giving me a really strong end, at least to this chapter. It was truly the best show day of my life.

While my front-row seat to Oprah Winfrey and all the good she puts into our world is now a seat in my living room just like every audience member I had the privilege of meeting, I still feel the impact of her words as if I'm sitting across the table from her or sitting in one of the famous red audience seats. For that, I will always be grateful.

Look for the part of your story that sticks with you, and start your story there. If you are struggling with where to start, say yes to the next unexpected invitation that comes your way—from your mother, your father or anyone who loves or likes you, and you just may find your story.

LOVESPEAKS LESSON #17: Love your story like it's your job. Speak your story. Your story is your stage. Your story is yours. And remember there is an audience for everyone. People are waiting to hear your story, so go out there and let your love speak!

Even though our stories never end, make sure you have a strong end for the chapter you are writing right now or speaking about on stage. It may not be a Smithsonian moment, but it's your moment, and that's what makes it your legacy and your story to tell.

What's your favorite full-circle story?

_____

_____

LOVESPEAKS PRACTICE: If you are accepting invitations from your mother, ask your mother to accept your invitations as well. Don't be shy about it. If you want people to say yes, let them know how much the invitation you are giving them matters to you. You have the power to get the yes you want, but only if you are upfront about it ... or resort to some lighthearted trickery!

Always look for a good end to a chapter of your story. Having my mom attend the *Watching Oprah* exhibit meant everything to me. Make your stories matter, and never give up on the ending you want.

ALTERNATIVE LOVESPEAKS PRACTICE: Say yes to anyone's invitation who loves or likes you. And remind them to accept yours. Mothers know best, but open your world of yes up to anyone who loves or likes you.

LIVE LOVESPEAKS: Just like speaking, invitations are a two-way street. If you want the people you love to accept your invitation, be a good guest and accept theirs. Just like being a good audience member for a speaker allows someone to be a good audience member for you, be a good guest.

Honor the person who gives you an invitation with a yes, and when you attend the event, arrive with a big fat smile on your face because invitations are to be celebrated. This is a gift we can all easily give people, and it costs nothing.

I could include a story right here for an example of what happens when someone finally says yes to your invitation, but I think it deserves its own chapter, and it feels good to end on chapter 18.

Is there something meaningful you desperately wanted that came back to you or something meaningful you want to come back to you?

_____

_____

_____

CHAPTER 18

It Will All Be Okay

*We are the authors of our own story and we have
the power to write the ending we want.*
—BRENÉ BROWN

Our stories never end, and neither does our work. I went to see my therapist on a particularly tough day recently when I experienced an unexpected setback from my husband's unresolved pain. And while I am a big fan of the unexpected, there are some unexpected things that are just not fun, kind of like unexpected turbulence.

I said to my therapist, "I've been working with you for six years, and today I feel like I'm right back where I started."

She looked at me with the most loving eyes and said, "No, you are not, Sally Lou. You are not at all where you started. You have done the work. You are strong. You will survive anything." And I believed her, but I was feeling very unsteady.

That night I woke up at three in the morning (of course) and felt the need to leave my house. I picked up my dog, Gracie, who was sleeping next to me, and put her in the car with me. I drove to Starbucks, and I sat in my car in the parking lot until it opened at five. Then I got my coffee, one of my most favorite pleasures, and I called my sister Cindy because it was six in the morning in New Jersey and I knew she'd be up. Cindy is always up.

We talked for an hour. I told her how much I hated when conversations ended because it meant I had to return to my pain. I had said the exact same thing to my therapist the day before when our session ended, and that was when my therapist said to me, "Have a conversation with God when you are alone, and you won't be lonely. Ask him for guidance and give him gratitude."

I know this. I already practice this. But it was advice I needed to really hear in this moment. Always the student.

Before I hung up with Cindy, she suggested I meditate before I went home, so I did. I was on day nine of *Oprah & Deepak's 21-Day Meditation Experience* titled "Manifesting Grace through Gratitude." I definitely needed some grace, and gratitude is always good for pain. Oprah's voice makes me feel so much love, and as you know, she always seems to meet me right where I am. I pulled up the meditation titled "Changing Your Personal Reality," and this is what Oprah said: "One of my favorite quotes is from Joseph Campbell. He says 'The privilege of a lifetime is being who you are.'"

I gasped. Immediately, I started crying. *Hello, God!* Of all the quotes to begin with in this unsteady moment. The quote I love the most. The quote that was painted on the wall of the west side of the Harpo building and that reminded me of my purpose daily. The quote I use in almost every single speech and workshop I give. The quote that I use in this book. The quote that is my mantra ... and now your mantra.

Oprah continued to speak about our connection to grace and how staying grounded in gratitude is our connection to the divine. Just like my therapist had suggested, I was feeling God and gratitude, a lesson I directly learned from the woman whose voice filled my car. Suddenly, I felt a lot less lonely.

Oprah went on to say, "You are the author of your own life story. You can start a new chapter any time you choose. So honor your authenticity, and live the story, your story, that no one else can live."

God showed up just like my therapist said God would. Every single word Oprah spoke infused me with power. My dog, Grace, was sitting beside me, reminding me that Grace is always welcome, the very reason why I chose her name.

I thanked God. I thanked Oprah. I thanked my therapist. I thanked Cindy. I thanked my dad. I thanked Gracie, and I sobbed buckets of gratitude alone in my car, but I felt a community of support around me.

Once again, Oprah's words reminded me that I have the power to change my circumstances, to have gratitude, and to love my story, even the shitty parts. This wasn't extra. This was God. I felt so much power return to my body and my soul. I felt my purpose, which meant I had no fear.

I have learned so much in my fifth decade. I've done the work and will continue to do the work, and I love myself way too much to settle for anything less. I am built on Team Oaksie and "That's my sister," and while

I will always put my hand out to help someone on my team and I will never leave a player on the field, I will always put my hand out to myself first.

A few days after my middle-of-the-night Starbucks run, I visited my grandfather's terra-cotta urns and saw that the sale sign said, Under Contract. My heart dropped. I emailed the owner of the house with my final invitation. I asked her to please consider selling the terra-cotta urns to me.

After I sent the email, I drove to Maple Street Park to talk to my dad because it was Sunday. It had been a tough week. I was questioning a lot, and I asked my dad to send me a sign that everything would be okay—a sign that was big enough for me to see and feel.

Six hours later the owner of the house in Wilmette emailed me to let me know their plan was to take one urn with them when they moved, but they would be happy to sell me the other urn, the urn I used to stick my head into when I was a little girl that made my voice powerful, the urn that was my home base.

Twenty-three years of putting this dream into the universe had finally paid off. My invitation to buy my grandfather's terra-cotta urn was accepted, and a piece of my childhood and my grandfather would return home to me. A piece of me would return as well, the piece that reminds me my voice and my story are powerful. My home base was back.

I have absolutely no place for this enormous terra-cotta urn since we no longer have a backyard, but I will find one. It's my work now to figure out if my grandfather's urn is a sign that it will all be okay or if it is a sign that I will be okay. I guess it really doesn't matter because all I asked of my dad was to send me a sign that it would all be okay. And so it will.

My husband is handling the logistics of the return of the terra-cotta urn like his story depends on it, and I can see his next chapter unfolding. I told him that if we can't fit this enormous urn on our small patio, we can put it in our garage and he can live in it. I'm just trying to keep the jokes fresh for my next chapter.

The following day I flew to Philadelphia to visit my mom. My trip had been planned for months, and I was really looking forward to spending time with her. As I boarded the plane, I made a last minute decision to listen to *Oprah & Deepak's 21-Day Meditation Experience.* I was now on day sixteen, and I wanted to hear more. It was risky because I have my boarding rituals of prayer, and listening to a meditation has never been part of my ritual.

As I walked down the Jetway, I heard Oprah's voice say, "One of my favorite experiences is when I'm flying in a plane and the plane begins to ascend."

I felt a smile cross my face. *Here we go!* She went on to say, "The secret of being lives in the moment you break through your own clouds."

Then my smile traveled from head to toes. My entire body was smiling. She ended by saying, "Suddenly you realize, 'Oh, right. This is what life is!' This is whole, safe, and powerful, and you feel like you're home. As Deepak will show us, grace brings you back to who you really are."

I felt my sail come up, straighter, stronger, and ready to press on. I felt my powerful voice speaking to me and saying, "I'm supposed to be here." And I boarded the plane with my dog Grace and absolutely no fear.

Speak. Love you story. Your audience is waiting.

LOVESPEAKS LESSON #18: Life is for the living, and my message to everyone reading this book is that it's not over and it will all be okay. Let lesson #18 remind you to live your life. Live it well. Let the hard parts remind you that you are alive and you can change your story.

I have lost a lot in the past few years—my house, my dad, my dog, some friends, my dream job, job opportunities, eight teeth, and almost my marriage. But I've also gained so much. I've gained me. I know exactly who I am, and I'm good with that.

I am happy to share with you that I finally did stand-up comedy, and I intend to do more. I haven't performed the first piece I wrote. That will take some time. I also received my level-one certification in Reiki healing. This is how I heal. I say yes to myself, which makes me a much better human for others.

Flip the script on how you see things. Instead of feeling what you have lost, discover what you can find. It's a beautiful lesson my friend Maleesa taught me that I try really hard to practice. Life is not guaranteed. What is guaranteed is that every damn day we are here is a gift. Be grateful for the opportunity to change what doesn't serve you or others and look for signs of love everywhere.

Surround yourself with people who love you and lift you up. Serve and protect the people you love and the things you love to do. Even if it's hard. Nothing matters more than this. Don't give up on the people you love who may be holding pain. Help them breakthrough. Help them find their purpose. Growth is uncomfortable, and that's okay.

Be fierce with your loyalty to those who bring you joy. Let your love speak for what matters most to you, but always be open to what matters to others as well. Remember everyone has a story.

Who reminds you that it will all be okay?

_____

_____

_____

LOVESPEAKS PRACTICE: Repeat to yourself, "It will all be okay," and it will. Look for the signs that accompany this mantra. On the recent fourth anniversary of my dad's death, I prayed for a sign from my father. Four hours later I woke up at four forty-two in the morning. There he was, literally waking me up to make sure I knew he was right there.

The next morning I went to O'Hare Airport and sat at a piano bar while I was waiting for my flight. The player piano started to play "Close to You." I smiled. The song that followed was "Raindrops Keep Falling on My Head." I watched the keys play back-to-back songs straight from my dad. It was as if he was sitting right there.

ALTERNATIVE LOVESPEAKS PRACTICE: Love yourself and you will be okay. I talk so much about thanking and loving the person who stands by you in life, but no one stands by you more than you. Give yourself the same love you give others. Put your hand out to yourself first. It will be a stronger hand to put out to others on your team when they need you.

LIVE LOVESPEAKS: I believe in God. I believe in good. I believe in the power of the universe.

The girl with the clipboard, my dad, my mom, my sisters, my grandparents, my grandfather's terra-cotta urns, my uncle Jody, Oprah, Brené Brown, John Travolta, 1021 Elm Street, my toboggan, my godfather, Dr. God, Dr. Love, my husband, my children, and all my angels on earth and in heaven were not sent to me by accident. They were sent to me with purpose. I honor their purpose every day of my life.

Just like my personality, my names were not given to me by accident. They were also given to me with purpose. I am a mighty oak who loves mankind and womankind.

It has been an honor for me to give you a peek inside my life. It's not perfect. None of our lives are. My kids keep saying, "Mom, you're not Beyoncé. You can't just write a book and tell your personal business like you're famous."

I tell them, "I don't want to be famous. I want to love my story, speak my story, and be a better human. I want to make people's lives better."

If any one little tiny sliver of my story impacts yours in a way that resonates with you and helps you with something you are struggling with and live a better life, I am grateful. And then I can tell my kids I did my job, and maybe they will think I am a rock star too. We all deserve to feel like rock stars. Today is your show day! And so is tomorrow. Go count your blessings, and start your story.

Each of the eighteen lessons and the eighteen journal pages are for you. Maybe you have written your words on these pages, and maybe you have spoken your words into the universe. It's time now for you to do the work—to love your story, to speak your story, to be a better human, to be a better speaker, to love yourself, and to share your story to help others heal and to heal yourself.

It is such a privilege to be you.

What part of your story have you shared to help others heal?

_____

_____

_____

Acknowledgments

Thank you to my husband for allowing me to share a part of my story that is hard for him to relive and for being brave enough to do the work in the most vulnerable and courageous way. Our work never ends, and neither do our stories.

Thank you to my children, Marin, Carly, and Billy, for being brave, for putting up with me, for believing in me, and for being the loves of my life. I am so grateful for your hearts and for teaching me to listen. I hear you because you matter most.

Thank you to my mom and dad for loving me unconditionally, for providing me with a rich childhood filled with stories, for teaching me to tell the truth, and for reminding me that I can do anything. Thank you to my dad for giving me my heart, and thank you to my mom for giving me my humor.

Thank you to my sisters Susan and Cindy for being my best friends, my number-one cheerleaders, my incredible role models, and my soft place to fall always.

Thank you to my mom mom for teaching me the importance of love, talent, strength, resilience, and community. Thank you to my nana for teaching me to love fashion, food, and entertaining. Thank you to my grandfather for also giving me my sense of humor, my attention to detail, and a terra-cotta urn that I speak into daily without any fear of being arrested.

Thank you to my uncle Jody for teaching me tolerance and unconditional love. Thank you to my aunt Sally Lou for teaching me grace. Thank you to my dogs Tinker and Gracie for being abundant sources of love.

Thank you to Oprah for giving me a stage to do what I love, for being the greatest human and teacher on earth and for changing my life forever.

Thank you to my brother-in-law Jud for taking care of the Oaks women as promised and for being the best brother I could ever have. Thank you to Stewart for being our unexpected gift. Thank you to all my delicious nieces, nephews, great-nieces, and great-nephews. Being an aunt is a role I love. Thank you to the Harteveldt, Loveman, and Cristal families for your love and support. A special thank you to Rob for your kindness. Thank you to Peter Cristal for the best dance of my life. We will finish in heaven.

Thank you to the Oaks women thread for giving me life and laughter—Mom, Cindy, Susan, Marin, Carly, Cammie, Madi, Lucy, Kristen, Lauren, and Kelly.

Thank you to my godfather Bill McCarter for being my mentor. Thank you to my talented godsister Amy McCarter for art-directing this book, naming my business, designing my lovespeaks graphics, sketching my tattoo, and designing my father's life celebration booklet. It has been such an added bonus of love to work with you on this passion project, knowing our dads are cheering us on above.

Thank you to the girl with the clipboard and *The Mike Douglas Show* for giving me my career in television.

Thank you to my small but mighty lovespeaks team—Julie Meute (my former Harpo teammate) for designing and managing my website, for running all the technical things I don't understand, and for always taking things to the next level; Aly Nauta for teaching me so much about branding and social media and for being my millennial must; Mary O'Donohue (another former Harpo teammate and founder of Mary O'Donohue Media) for her kindness and coaching. And to my publicist Abby Dunn, whose mantra should be "Done and Dunn!"

Thank you also to a talented group of women author friends—Lee Woodruff, Linda Gartz, Kelley Kitley, Amy Kite, Chrishaunda Lee Perez, Val Gangas, and Sarah Victory—for being beautiful writers and inspiring me to write my story.

Thank you to Amanda Wurzbach, Linda Bergonia, and Annie Wasserman, who each helped me launch my brand. Thank you to Nancy Shaw, who wrote my entire brand on a cocktail napkin.

Thank you to my Harpo audience team for being my family, my lifeline, and my best audience. I'm so proud of all the talent you are all putting out into the world Sharvo, Teresa, Julie, Sherry, Dana, Andy, both Mark Ps, Nicole, Becky, Itika, and Ellie, your success is my joy.

Thank you to my Harpo family for all the love, for the referrals, and for making me always strive to be better. Thank you the most to Harriet Seitler for saying the four words that saved me—I love you forever. Thank you to Irma Norris for your mentorship and letting me do what I love.

Thank you to *The Oprah Winfrey Show* audience for giving me the time of my life and for supporting me in my business. Thank you to my lovespeaks peeps who have attended my workshops, speeches, and events, referred business to me, and loved or liked me on social media. Hopefully, you are reading this book!

Thank you to the *TODAY* team for treating me like one of your own and making me feel valued, especially Alex and Sam. I miss you daily.

Thank you to Brené Brown for *Daring Greatly* and the *Courage Works* course, which gave me the courage to heal and write this book. Thank you to Beyoncé for reminding us all that women run the world. Thank you to Michelle Obama for *Becoming* and for being superwoman.

Thank you to the late Ray Farkas for telling me about the Irving B. Harris Internship. Thank you to Dave Johnson, my Lafayette College English professor, for encouraging me to apply to the internship that would bring me to a city that would change my life. Thank you to the Harris Internship Committee—Pat, Fran, Andy, and Libbet—for choosing me.

Thank you to Marcy Cole, Henry Robin, Bob McGarity, Andrea Josephson Sullivan, and Peter Sullivan for your hearts and for providing such good content and making life way more fun. Thank you to Betsy Graham Tilkemeier and Kelsey Drowne Leachman for being my best friends for life. Thank you to Karen Stein Solomon for being beside me all the way.

Thank you to Gia Amato Miller for your unconditional love and for being my soul sister; Diane Maegher for thirty-five years of friendship and for always asking me how I am; Gayle Teicher for your positivity and wheatgrass shots; Lisa Ripka for being the glue; Leslie Herpin for your Southern comfort; and Cindy Mogentale for being a dedicated source of so much support. Thank you to Kelly Styne for your lovespeaks art.

Thank you to my Lafayette College family, especially Leigh & Leidy Smith, Evan Deoul, Betsy Phillips, Ellen Weiler, Sandy Kazinski, Karen Ziegler Kelly and Caroline Bitterly for being my leopard pack. Thank you to the Lafayette men's soccer community for being my father's friends, especially Jim "Benji" Benjamin, David "Woody" Fryman, and George Tiger. Thank you to Lafayette College and its community for being a place my family calls home.

Thank you to the Cynwyd Clowns and their families who were such a rich part of my childhood.

Thank you to my network of women supporting women—Rita Coburn, Jill Frank, Kathleen Sarpy, Whitney Reynolds, Maleesa Xiong, Vicki Reece,

Mona Antwan, Bela Gandhi Val Haller, Leslie Bond, Danielle Robay, Dina Engler, Kathy Taslitz, Sharon Graboys, Diana Divine, Lauren Laughlin, Lauren Sara, Jill Alberts, Erica Ayala, Laura Lederer, Cathy Ross, Alyssa Burns, Eyde Gershman, Joan Deoul, Izzy Cross, Cécile Pochet, Jen Ublasi, Julie Melulis, Denise Hamburger, Kelley Long Nayak, Kelly and Katrina Henderson, Kristy Harteveldt, Susan Hagaman, Julie Cristal, Susan Cristal, Barbara Best and every woman's name mentioned in this acknowledgement. Your support means the world to me.

Thank you to my new friend Michelle Sorro for lighting a fire in me and reminding me to do what I love. Thank you to Julius Graham for being my number-one lovespeaks fan and for pushing me when I needed it most.

Thank you to Brittani Sylvester and Teodora Boboc for your hearts and letting my love speak on your table while you tried to make me beautiful. Thank you to Mona Sapper, Kate Kaczowka, Kathy Eshoo and Vivan Arpino for doing the same in your chair. And thank you to Dr. Lorri for being my best audience. You will never know how much your laughter healed me.

Thank you to my periodontist, Dr. Nolan Levine, for giving me an opportunity to be still in your chair and manifest lovespeaks in between the needles, drills, extractions, stitches, and ice packs. Thank you to my dentist, Dr. Sergio Rubenstein, for giving me my new teeth because speakers need teeth!

Thank you to our healing team Dr. God, Carol, Daniel, Rabbi Steve, Christopher, Elisa, and Christine for literally saving us and for being our spiritual glue.

Thank you to Carla and Duncan Brown for teaching me and my family transcendental meditation. Thank to Margo Kellison Lightburn for introducing me to yoga and your healing voice.

Thank you to Maple Street Park for giving me a place to visit with my dad. Thank you to Kathy and Bob Bernstein for returning my grandfather's terra-cotta urn to me and for not arresting me. Thank you also for allowing us to put good into the universe by supporting your family's charity Guitars over Guns in return for the urn. I like the way you do business!

Thank you to my hometown Gladwyne, Pennsylvania, where I was so privileged to grow up. Thank you to Tower Beach and Lake Michigan for your healing waters. Thank you to the Jersey Shore for your sand, your salt, your cool breezes, and Bruce Springsteen.

Thank you to my team at Balboa Press beginning with Marsha who when she told me I would be a published author I wanted to jump through the phone and hug her! Thank you to Mary Oxley and Scott Crenshaw for getting me through the whole process. And thank you to the Balboa design, production and marketing teams for moving at my pace! Thank you.

To anyone who has ever sat in a TV studio audience when I was on the stage or to members of the lovespeaks audience, you give me life. I would never be the speaker I am today without you because as you know, *the better the audience, the better the speaker*. Now that I am an author, my hope is that the better the reader, the better the writer! To anyone who has taken the time to read this book, thank you. Your love speaks!

And finally, thank you to God for giving me the courage to be who I am and walk in your way.

Glossary

Show day:	**TRANSFORMING LIVES.**
I'm on my way:	**I LOVE YOU.**
That's my sister:	**PROTECT THE PEOPLE YOU LOVE.**
Don't tilt the boxes:	**CARE FOR YOUR TALENT.**
You have great hair:	**YOU'RE DOING GREAT.**
Accept invitations from your mother:	**START YOUR STORY.**
Say do you remember:	**SALLY LOU, REMEMBER?**
Mom, give me my pipe:	**A MIX-UP.**
Thanks for the Lou:	**YOU KNOW ME.**
18:	**LIFE.**
Storytelling:	**SAVES LIVES.**
The '80s are over:	**LIFE WILL NEVER BE AS GOOD.**
Phantasmagorical:	**THE BEST OF THE VERY, VERY BEST.**

Ten Lovespeaks Lessons to Live By

1.
Do what you love.
2.
Work in an environment that
pleases all five of your senses.
3.
Own your talent, and share your talent.
4.
Give compliments.
5.
Unexpectedly connect with your
audience on the stage and off.
6.
Speak the truth.
7.
Love your story like it's your job.
8.
Accept invitations from your mother
or anyone who loves or likes you.
9.
Bring people onto your team who don't look
like you, act like you, or think like you.
10.
Practice meditation.

Worth 1,000 Words

MY PARENTS SPEAK

1.

2.

3.

MY SISTERS SPEAK

4.

5.

1. My dad was always running—1952   2. My parents fell in love at the Jersey Shore—1950   3. My mom holding me—1963   4. Trying to be one of "the girls"—1966   5. Beach football was a family sport—1968

MY FOUNDATION SPEAKS

1.
2.
3.

4.
5.

MY CHILDHOOD SPEAKS

6.
7.

1. My nana and pop pop—1970s   2. My mom mom—1960s   3. My uncle Jody at my parents' wedding—1954   4. My grandfather's terra-cotta urn that made my voice powerful—1980s   5. The ticket that changed my life—1976   6. Me and Betsy at Stony Lane Swim Club—1971   7. My favorite Bar/Bat Mitzvah outfit—1975

MY CHICAGO SPEAKS

1.

2.

3.

MY SHOW DAY SPEAKS

4.
5.

6.

1. My parents drove me to Chicago in my Subaru—1984   2. Me and Oprah at a holiday party—1987   3. I prepared our audience check-in list on this typewriter every night—1987   4. Marin and Carly on *The Oprah Winfrey Show* 1999, © Harpo Inc./George Burns   5. Doing the warm-up at *The Oprah Winfrey Show*— 2010, © Harpo Inc./George Burns   6. Billy running camera at *The Oprah Winfrey Show*—2009, © Harpo Inc./George Burns

MY DNA SPEAKS

MY TEAM SPEAKS

1. Marin and her clipboard at *TODAY*—2015   2. Billy doing what he loves—2017   3. The girl with the clipboard and Oprah—approximately 2006, © Harpo Inc./George Burns   4. Carly and her clipboard at *Windy City Live*—2016   5. Team Oaksie celebrating my dad's eightieth birthday at Oaks Stadium—2008   6. Me and my audience team—2011, © Harpo Inc./George Burns

MY MAGIC SPEAKS

1.

2.

3.

4.

MY CIRCLE SPEAKS

5.

6.

1. Our family photo with Oprah on the trip to Hawaii—2006, © Harpo Inc./ Robin Layton   2. Me probably saying "fanny" in Sydney, Australia—2011, © Harpo Inc./George Burns   3. Me pretending to be brave on the Sydney Harbor Bridge—2011   4. Me warming up the audience at the United Center—2011, © Harpo Inc./George Burns   5. The Lafayette College 9—2014   6. My Oaks family circle keeps me mighty and strong—2019

MY HEART SPEAKS

1.

2.

3.
4.

5.

MY FRIENDS SPEAK

1. My parents toasting to love—2012   2. Our sweet Gracie because grace is always welcome—2016   3. My kids are my everything—2018   4. Me visiting my grandfather's terra-cotta urns in Wilmette—2013   5. We dress alike and laugh a lot—2018   6. Me, Marcy and Henry—2017   7. Me and Andrea—2013   8. Me and Betsy—2015

MY SIGNS SPEAK

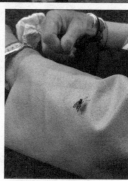

MY PURPOSE SPEAKS

1. The letter my dad wrote me on May, 23 2011   2. Seeing the last truck in the J. J. Skelton fleet during a Christmas visit in Gladwyne—2012   3. My dad's adorable face—2014   4. My dad holding my cross—2015   5. My bee visitors—2015   6. Speaking on a plane with no fear—2017   7. Seeing Bruce Springsteen on Broadway— 2018   8. Me and my mom at the *Watching Oprah* exhibit at the National Museum of African American History and Culture—2018

MY MOMENTUM SPEAKS

1.
2.
3.
4.

MY LOVE SPEAKERS SPEAK

5.
6.
7.

8.
9.

1. Everybody gets a brick!—2012   2. My husband and I moving forward—2013   3. When all else fails, I can still throw a football—2017   4. A tribute to my dad on the thirteenth step at Oaks Stadium—2016   5. Kathleen Sarpy, founder and CEO of Agency H5—2019, © Jules Kennedy   6. Mona Antwan, founder of Mindfulness Leader—2019, © Jules Kennedy   7. Rita Coburn, founder of RCW Media Productions—2019, © Jules Kennedy   8. Bela Gandhi, founder of Smart Dating Academy—2019, © Jules Kennedy   9. Whitney Reynolds, host and owner of *The Whitney Reynolds Show*—2019, © Jules Kennedy

MY LOVE SPEAKERS SPEAK

1.
2.
3.
4.
5.

MY LOVE SPEAKS

6.
7.
8.

1. Maleesa Xiong is a self-described creative doer and explorer—2019, © Jules Kennedy   2. Jill Frank, head of content productions at Epsilon—2019, © Jules Kennedy   3. Vicki Reece, founder of Joy of Mom—2019, © Jules Kennedy   4. Val Haller, founder of ValsList—2018, © Cynthia Lynn Photography   5. Amy McCarter, founder of McCarter Design, Chicago and art director of *SPEAK*—2019, © 2017 dimitre.com   6. So many of my stories are rooted in this red seat—2019, © Aly Nauta   7. I always leave room for the unexpected—2019, © Aly Nauta   8. Love on!—2019, © Jules Kennedy

1 | The Unexpected Speaker

I am not normal and I want to help you not be
normal too, because normal is so expected.
—S. L. L.

———

- Don't let labels define me. Let them inspire me
  - When I am in my purpose, I have no fear.
- Speaking is like everything I do. It's a practice.

———

Here are some thoughts around letting go of fear and being unexpected.

_____

_____

_____

_____

_____

_____

_____

_____

_____

_____

_____

_____

_____

_____

2 | A Little Bit of Extra Love Goes a Long Way

My story is my comfort, my joy and my security,
including the parts that are ugly and painful.
—S. L. L.

———

- My story connects me to others.
- Storytelling makes me a better human.
- My story is my platform.

———

Here are some thoughts around loving my story.

_____

_____

_____

_____

_____

_____

_____

_____

_____

_____

_____

_____

3 | Accept Invitations from Your Mother

Lame excuses are lame. They add nothing extra to
our stories. Say yes to your mother's invitation.
—S. L. L.

———

- I will say yes to invitations from anyone who loves or likes me with no expectations.
- I will define my talent.
- I will share my talent with others.

———

Here are some thoughts around accepting invitations and owning my talent.

_____

_____

_____

_____

_____

_____

_____

_____

_____

_____

_____

_____

_____

4 | I'm Sensing a Story

*Connecting our talents to the careers we choose
makes us all so much more efficient and reduces time
wasted trying to figure out who we want to be.*
—S. L. L.

———

- I will find a career that pleases all five of my senses.
- I will do what I love.
- I will spend more time in the environment I love.

———

Here are some thoughts around using my five senses.

_____

_____

_____

_____

_____

_____

_____

_____

_____

_____

_____

_____

_____

5 | Don't Tilt the Boxes

*I may not make pretty tea sandwiches, but my hope is that
the community I have created through my business feels
as much love when they see me on a stage, at an event, on
Facebook, Instagram, or in their in-box, as my grandmother's
customers felt when they arrived at her door.*
—S. L. L.

———

- My team can't look like me, act like me, or think like me.
  - I will build my community.
  - I will care for my craft.

———

Here are some thoughts around caring for my craft and connecting with my community.

_____

_____

_____

_____

_____

_____

_____

_____

_____

_____

_____

6 | From Great Oaks Little Acorns Grow

Find a way to unexpectedly bless someone with kindness.
—S. L. L.

———

- I will be kind.
- I will work hard.
- I will be kind to myself when I am told no and watch for the gift that is on its way.

———

Here are some thoughts around kindness.

_____

_____

_____

_____

_____

_____

_____

_____

_____

_____

_____

_____

_____

_____

_____

_____

7 | Living Lovespeaks

I treat every day like 'The Oprah Winfrey Show' audience warm-up, whether I am on a stage or off of a stage. Practice your timing and wit on the people who surround you in your life. See them. Hear them. Celebrate them. And if you're lucky, make them laugh.
—S. L. L.

———

- I will be brave in my life and let that power serve me when I speak.
- Before I speak, I will repeat, "I'm supposed to be here."
- When I speak, I will use an unexpected speaker move to connect with my audience.

———

Here are some thoughts on letting love speak.

_____

_____

_____

_____

_____

_____

_____

_____

_____

_____

_____

8 | Stories from the Red Seat

Magic is not reserved for 'The Oprah Winfrey Show;' magic is reserved for anyone who is willing to see it and embody it.
—*S. L. L.*

———

- I will look for magic everywhere.
  - I will make magic.
- I will find a boss who inspires me.

———

Here are some thoughts around finding magic and making magic.

_____

_____

_____

_____

_____

_____

_____

_____

_____

_____

_____

_____

_____

_____

_____

_____

_____

9 | Love Your Audience

Give your audience love by listening to them and let them know they matter. Whether you are a speaker, an influencer, or a leader of a company or nonprofit, know that fans, clients, customers, and employees are all audiences. There is an audience for everyone, and yours is waiting.
—S. L. L.

———

- I will listen to others.
- I will ask for someone to listen to me.
- I will make someone's life better today.

———

Here are some thoughts around listening.

_____

_____

_____

_____

_____

_____

_____

_____

_____

_____

_____

10 | Does Anyone Even Like Me?

Turn up the volume in your life by staying
connected to the people who like you.
—S. L. L.

———

- I am enough.
- I will love my people.
- My words have power.

———

Here are some thoughts on liking who I am.

_____

_____

_____

_____

_____

_____

_____

_____

_____

_____

_____

_____

_____

_____

11 | Faith Is Cheaper than Botox

We are all looking to be inspired by someone who leads us to work harder, heal faster, make better choices and live in our truth.
—*S. L. L.*

———

- I will speak my truth.
- I will look for the open door.
- I will look for people to inspire me to live my truth.

———

Here are some thoughts around speaking my truth.

_____

_____

_____

_____

_____

_____

_____

_____

_____

_____

_____

_____

_____

_____

12 | The Unexpected Thank-You

*Forgiveness is the greatest gift you can give yourself. It is a gift
of self-love. It's a gift that allows you to keep being who you
are without having to give up a piece of your identity.*
—S. L. L.

———

- I will forgive myself.
- I will consider someone else's story.
- I will speak in compound sentences.

———

Here are some thoughts on forgiveness.

_____

_____

_____

_____

_____

_____

_____

_____

_____

_____

_____

_____

_____

13 | The Universe Is Calling. Don't Hang Up.

When people or things you love show up in your life, take them as signs you are on the right path and that everything will be okay.
—*S. L. L.*

———

- I will open my eyes and my heart to the universe and look for signs of love.
- I will visualize the story I want to write.
- I will enjoy the lessons when they comes full circle.

———

Here are some thoughts around taking the call from the universe.

_____

_____

_____

_____

_____

_____

_____

_____

_____

_____

_____

14 | The Unexpected You

You are your most important audience.
—S. L. L.

———

- I will invest in myself.
- I will put myself first on my list.
- I will take some time for mindfulness.

———

Here are some thoughts around making time for me.

_____

_____

_____

_____

_____

_____

_____

_____

_____

_____

_____

_____

_____

15 | I'm on My Way

Life is for the living. Tell your people you love them. Let your love speak!
—S. L. L.

————

- I will keep the people I love close to me.
- I will take time to let my love speak.
- I will say I love you to the people I love.

————

Here are some thoughts around keeping close to the people I love.

_____

_____

_____

_____

_____

_____

_____

_____

_____

_____

_____

_____

_____

_____

16 | Love Never Leaves

We may lose someone we love, but they never leave our lives. That's the unexpected gift.
—S. L. L.

———

- Death does not separate me from people I love because love never leaves.
- I will practice staying connected to people I have lost.
- I will reach out to someone I love whom I haven't connected with recently.

———

Here are some thoughts around connecting with someone I have lost.

_____

_____

_____

_____

_____

_____

_____

_____

_____

_____

_____

_____

17 | Accept Invitations from Your Daughter

*Even though our stories never end, make sure you have a strong
end for the chapter you are experiencing or speaking about.*
—S. L. L.

———

- When an invitation is important to me, I will tell the person I'm inviting how much his or her yes means.
  - There is an audience for me.
- I will look for strong endings to each of my chapters.

———

Here are some thoughts around the chapter of my story I am writing today.

_____

_____

_____

_____

_____

_____

_____

_____

_____

_____

_____

_____

_____

18 | It Will All Be Okay

Let lesson #18 remind you to live your life. Live it well. Let the hard parts remind you that you are alive and you can change your story.
—*S. L. L.*

———

- I am here, and I can change my story.
- I will practice gratitude and grace.
- It will all be okay.

———

Here are some thoughts about changing my story.

_____

_____

_____

_____

_____

_____

_____

_____

_____

_____

_____

_____

_____

_____

Congratulations!

You have your story ... and maybe even your book. Your love speaks!